Doesn't It Hurt?
Confessions of Compulsive Hair Pullers

Edited by
Sandy Rosenblatt

DEDICATION

To all those who have ever lived with trichotillomania

CONTENTS

FORWARD

Statistics show that 1 in 50 Americans have trichotillomania. However, the real number of those with trich may be much higher. Many people are too embarrassed or ashamed to admit they pull their hair and go to great lengths to hide their behavior from family, friends, and medical professionals.

Those of us with trich can often feel broken and alone. We want to tell people we're hurting, but we're afraid of what they'll say. We're afraid they'll reject us. We're afraid because in a way, we reject ourselves.

We suffer for years because we're scared to share that we pull out our hair. We spend countless hours trying to hide or cover the area where we've pulled. We desperately hope no one will notice and want to avoid a negative reaction, but at the very same time, we judge ourselves for it. This impacts both our mental and spiritual health, as well as our relationships with others. Worst of all, it destroys our faith in ourselves.

I created this book because there simply isn't anything like it. Very few books chronicle people's personal experiences with trich (not psychological analyses). And while there are many blogs, Facebook and Twitter pages dedicated to the subjective experience of having trich, there's no one place one can go to read a collection of stories all in one place.

This type of vulnerability can be daunting to reveal, because we never know how someone will react to our truth. However, when we are unable to speak our truth and keep it locked away, we also hold on to the shame. This shame (not the pulling itself) is what cuts us off from how we really want to show up in the world.

I created this book to show others that in sharing our stories, we can feel proud and confident. There is power in sharing our journey. Whether we still pull out our hair or we've stopped, we can tell our stories and show ourselves self-love in the process. We can honor our truth and own our true selves. We can find beauty in who we are.

I also wanted to create a place in which we are safe to share our stories, all together. There is healing not only for those of us who are open about having trich, but for others, who will finally be able to admit that they, too, have been there, have felt what we have felt. I wanted them to reclaim this dignity, and to be able to do so from the privacy of their own home. I wanted to create a vehicle for us to feel connected to one other, as well as educate those unfamiliar with what it is actually like to live with trichotillomania.

This book was a collaborative effort. Within one week of deciding to go ahead with the project, I found 14 others who were willing to openly and authentically contribute their personal stories. For some, this is the first time they've opened up. They've never before disclosed that they have trich, and I am honored that they chose to do so within the confines of this book.

The contributors are both women and men. We hail from five different countries. We range in age from 18 to mid-60s. We are teachers, students, non-profit professionals, medical professionals, and executive directors. Some of us are married with children while others are single. We are mothers, fathers and someone's child. Some of us are well-known trich advocates, and some of us have never spoken publicly about having the disorder. Some of us still pull our hair from different areas of our bodies, and some of us have stopped. We are as diverse as you.

And no matter who we are, we're here to remind you that you are never really alone.

Sandy Rosenblatt, Editor

1
KICKING TRICH'S ASS
KATHERINE, LATE TEENS, NEW YORK

No matter how well I write my story I've come to the conclusion that a person cannot fully understand trichotillomania unless they've laid in bed at 2 a.m. covered in hair, painfully aware of their throbbing scalp. However, it's crucial for those suffering from trichotillomania to talk about their experiences, not only to educate society, but also to help other trichsters feel less alone.

Trichotillomania is about so much more than hair, or lack thereof. It can be socially crippling and certainly emotionally exhausting, and yet, I wouldn't trade my experience with trichotillomania for the world. Like many sufferers, I started pulling my hair out at the peak of adolescence. I can vividly remember the first time I pulled out my hair. Of course, I could have been pulling before this point unconsciously, but I'll never know for sure. I was around twelve years old and heading to Florida for a vacation along with my mom, younger brother, and close family friends. It was supposed to be a relaxing and fun-filled week with friends and family. I don't remember a single detail of the vacation except that as each day went by the spot where my hair parted grew thinner and thinner. Right before vacation I had gotten bangs for the first time and bleach blonde highlights. I was standing in front of the illuminated mirror looking at the small imperfections on my skin and examining my bangs thoroughly to see if all the hairs were even in length. Suddenly I noticed one dark hair, which was slightly longer than all the others, and promptly plucked it from my scalp.

Little did I know that I had just started something that would change the course of my life forever.

Something that still leaves me in awe is how nonchalantly I pulled that first hair. I found nothing wrong with ripping the strand from my head; I assumed everyone did that when they had hairs out of place. For the remainder of the vacation I pulled individual strands of hair as if it was no big deal. Eventually my mom noticed my hand constantly going to my head and began finding the strands of hair all over the couch and my bed. She panicked, saying she had seen something about this on a medical show. When she said there was something wrong with my "hair pulling habit" I laughed at her and insisted I was absolutely fine. Nevertheless, once we got home from that vacation she began doing her own online investigation of the topic. She never showed me what she found while she was researching, but it was enough to make her take me to a local dermatologist.

Now we've probably all had a bad experience at a doctor's office, but my ordeal might just take the cake. I don't blame my mom for taking me to this doctor; I mean what are you supposed to do when your kid starts pulling out their hair? Where do you go? All I know is that this was my first encounter with the absolute ignorance of my condition. When my name was called in the waiting room I walked into the room with my mom and was greeted by a young, attractive nurse. I remember thinking her long dark hair was gorgeous. She started off by asking basic questions like height and weight before she finally got to the kicker, "Why are you here today?"

I could feel myself struggling to answer but finally blurted out, "I keep pulling out my hair." The look of horror and disgust that washed over her face was something that will be forever engraved in my mind. I immediately felt embarrassed and the judgment in her voice felt like daggers when she exclaimed, "Well why don't you just stop?!" I tried to explain to her that I couldn't stop. It wasn't that simple. She finished taking down my information, and I held back the tears that I knew were inevitable.

As soon as she walked out of the room I began hysterically crying and asking my mom to take me home. I didn't have much time to dry my eyes before the doctor came in and began looking over the notes the nurse had taken down. The rest of the appointment was a blur and to be honest I tuned out most of it. In the end I was diagnosed with trichotillomania via a Wikipedia article the doctor found when he Googled hair pulling. I left that office feeling more alone and isolated than you could possibly imagine. I now knew this "hair pulling habit" had a name, but I didn't know much else about it. I felt like the only person in the world who did this to herself. All I could feel was frustration with myself and with the world. If a doctor couldn't even understand what was wrong with me how could I expect my friends and family to understand? Hell, I didn't even understand it myself!

My first few months after being diagnosed were some of the most difficult. I searched drastically for answers that were nowhere to be found. Of course my mom was also searching for answers and in the process told tons of people about my hair pulling problem. This is when the tension between us first started to arise. I had realized by then that people didn't take well to my habit and thought of me differently once they found out about my problem. I was beyond pissed off at my mom for telling people about my hair pulling; after all it wasn't her secret to tell. When my parents realized the problem wasn't simply going to vanish on its' own, they decided to take me to a local counseling center. I fought going to therapy for as long as I could because I assumed if I gave in to therapy I also gave in to the idea that I was crazy.

The first therapist I went to was a young woman named Samantha who knew nothing of trichotillomania and spent most of our sessions discussing friends and family life. She was nice enough and made me feel comfortable with the idea of therapy but there was no improvement in my pulling. There is only one thing I remember vividly about my sessions with Samantha and that is how she was the first one to notice my early signs of depression. After not being able to say anything positive about myself she told me to stand in front of the mirror in the office bathroom until I could identify one trait I liked. I spent three entire sessions standing in front of that mirror and was never able to say anything good about myself; instead I critiqued my body and personality until I filled up with self-hatred and began crying uncontrollably.

From there my parents decided to try a psychiatrist who had come highly recommended and supposedly treated trichotillomania before. He was an older man who was very soft spoken and had a big fancy office. After my initial evaluation he explained to me that if I were put on the correct mixture of medications I would easily stop pulling my hair. At the time I had no idea that there is no "cure" for trichotillomania and that many times medications don't help or only help slightly. This doctor gave me so much false hope that when the medications continued to do nothing I became even more depressed than before. Not to mention, I was a 13 year-old girl taking an obscene amount of anti-depressants. Foggy isn't even the right way to describe how I felt, I was completely out of it for most of that year. So after my parents finally realized the medication wasn't working, I was carted off to lots of other psychologists and psychiatrists. To be honest I can't even remember the names of all the doctors I saw. There must have been upwards of a dozen. All the while my hair was getting thinner by the day and I had to find new ways to cover up the bald spots.

At first I pulled my hair strand by strand and usually stuck to a single patch of hair at a time. Wearing my hair in a high ponytail or wearing a thick headband over the bald patches easily covered this. Slowly but surely I began pulling more hairs at a time, and before I knew it I was pulling fistfuls from all over my head. By the middle of eighth grade I had no choice but to wear hats every day to cover my balding head.

One of the more difficult parts of having trichotillomania in middle school was dealing with my peers and so-called friends. An important lesson I learned throughout my experience with trich is that people tended to judge what they didn't understand. This definitely holds true for 13 and 14-year old kids.

Since hats weren't generally allowed in my school, everyone wanted to know why I was allowed to wear one. Kids became overly curious and started trying to figure out why I was getting special privileges. After a social studies test one day my best friend came up to me and explained that everyone had watched me pull out my hair from under my hat during the entire test. I hadn't even realized I was pulling, but as I looked back at my desk I saw the huge clump of hair on the floor right next to it. From then on I got constant stares from random people in the hallways and people whispered as I walked by. Nothing bothered me more than the whispers and pointing. They didn't even have the respect to say it to my face!

Instead they snickered things like "what the heck is wrong with that freak?" right in front of me, as if pulling my hair came with hearing loss as well. The toughest blow was when my best friend since preschool no longer wanted to be seen with me in public. I was kicked out of my lunch table and began bringing my lunch to the library and eating by myself. I closed myself off from the world and spent most of my time alone in my room. I slept as often as I could because I hated the reality I faced when I was awake. My world was being swallowed up by darkness and self-pity. I was engulfed in depression at this point in my life.

The end of eighth grade was the first time I spoke publicly about my trichotillomania. I went to a teacher who I admired and asked her to tell the other kids in my class to stop bullying me. She suggested that perhaps if I explained the condition to them more, they would stop mocking me. Figuring I had nothing left to lose, I stood in front of my science class and explained that trichotillomania is a medical condition, and that I was no different than any one of them. I just had less hair on my head. I threw out the few facts I knew about trich, like that it had no known "cure." Some of my peers apologized for their previous cruel remarks, but others continued to harass me and treat me like an absolute freak of nature. Sadly, I began to see myself as a freak as well. They say the more you hear something, the more likely you are to believe it, and so by the end of eighth grade I had convinced myself that I was a horrible human being who didn't deserve sympathy or kindness from others.

That summer I retreated into my room and stayed locked there for most of my time. The few times people called looking for me I made excuses that I was busy, when in reality I was sleeping or staring at the walls of my room feeling like they were closing in on me. On top of all my internal conflict, my relationship with my mother was continuously deteriorating and there was plenty of external conflict as well. She had always been a controlling person, telling me how much makeup to wear, how to dress, and she even fixed my hair for me until I started pulling it out of my scalp. All my life I felt a certain pressure to be the perfect daughter, but I never expressed it to her. Now suddenly I was a wreck, and I felt like she was ashamed of me. I remember thinking to myself, "When did perfect little Katherine get so screwed up?"

There is nothing worse than seeing your parent cry. Knowing you are the cause of their sadness makes it even worse. On several occasions she came to me in absolute hysterics with fistfuls of my hair that she had cleaned off the floor. She begged me to stop, she told me she loved me and that I shouldn't be doing this to myself, but nothing she said helped. Nothing anyone said helped. At first her disappointment and sadness made me sad too, but then I got angry. In fact I became nothing short of enraged. Did she really care that I was suffering from this condition or did she just care what the neighbors thought? Didn't she understand that if I could just stop I would?

The fact that nobody understood how I felt, as much as they tried, became my biggest frustration. That summer I made the decision to go to a Catholic high school instead of returning to my public school where I knew I would be shunned once again. I saw high school as an opportunity for a fresh start, and I prayed that people would be kind. However, I made the decision to hide my condition at all costs. So the first step was to buy a wig and hope that no one would notice it was a wig. Buying my wig brought me so much happiness at first, but eventually it became such a burden to hide my hair pulling secret. High school was great in the beginning! I even made friends, told a select few about my condition, and they were really supportive.

13

Despite my new friends, school became more difficult and my depression got worse with every passing week. Every bad grade, every fight with my mom, every morning I put on my wig, I fell deeper into the dark hole. Any resemblance of the happy person I was before trichotillomania had vanished completely. The only people who ever witnessed me without my wig were the girls on my local church basketball team. I wore a bandana over my now totally bald scalp so I wouldn't sweat under my wig. The girls all assumed I was a cancer patient and as horrible as this may sound, I let them continue to think it. At least if they thought I had cancer I would get sympathy instead of judgments and glares.

I kept waiting for life to get better, but I couldn't help but feel like I was drowning in my own sadness. The best way I can describe it is being locked in a room that is continuously filled up with water and no matter how hard you try to keep your head above it, you know you'll eventually drown. The days started blending together and when I would lie in bed at the end of a school day, I couldn't remember a single detail. My entire life became an out of body experience. My eyes felt glazed over and I seemed to be trudging through a fog everyday. I knew something was seriously wrong when I couldn't even feel sadness anymore. I was fully numb. Sometimes the feeling of a hair ripped from my head was enough to bring me back to reality, but when it wasn't, I started turning to a knife for relief.

Many people neglect to discuss their experiences with depression or self-harm when talking about trichotillomania, but for me they went hand-in-hand. By my sophomore year of high school I was overcome by feelings of hopelessness. Just going through day-to-day life made me absolutely exhausted. At some point I stopped trying to fake a smile and accepted the fact that I had lost myself. I don't remember the first time thoughts of ending my life entered my mind, but I know that once I let those thoughts in they only grew stronger. I thought I was a waste of space, taking up room that someone else could be enjoying in this world. I saw the strain I was putting on my family, between my mood swings and my hair pulling, I was more trouble than I was worth. To top it off I knew my family would be financially better off without me, not having to pay for doctors or medications that never worked. When I pictured the world without me I saw my family happy and stable once again. I saw my friends, who would be a little upset at first, but after a few months they would forget about me and move on with life. They would graduate and go to college. Perhaps get married. Maybe someday they would think back on "that girl who pulled her hair out," but nothing more.

The world I pictured was bright and optimistic without me in it. Besides, I couldn't picture a future for myself and on the rare occasions that

I did, I didn't like what I saw. I imagined trying to date with trichotillomania, but let's face it, who wants the bald girlfriend? I pictured living alone in college because what roommate in their right mind would deal with finding clumps of hair all over the dorm? On the off chance I got married, I saw myself walking down the aisle wearing a wig and sporting scars all over my wrists. I could see no way to go on living. The room had completely filled with water, and I was finally drowning.

I started planning out my own death. Pills seemed too comfortable. I wanted to suffer. For some reason I was convinced that my hair pulling had caused all the problems in the world around me, and I deserved to feel pain for all the pain I had caused others. While other students doodled on their papers after finishing tests, I was writing out my own suicide note. One night after a bad day of pulling and a screaming match with my mom, I decided to see how deep I could cut.

With a razor and box opener I tore myself open and didn't stop until my mom came upstairs to find me. When she asked if I was trying to kill myself, I lied and said no. Truthfully I didn't want to die, I just wanted all the chaos in my life to stop. I wanted to feel happiness again. I wanted the voices in my head screaming that I wasn't good enough to be silenced. I didn't know any other way out.

It was late and my mom looked me in the eyes and said, "If I leave you alone to go to sleep can I trust that you won't try to kill yourself tonight?" I wanted so badly to tell her I'd be fine, but I knew that would be a lie. Deep down I was aware that as soon as she left me alone I would finish what I had started. I couldn't bring myself to say what we both already knew, so I sat there shaking my head and wiping the blood on my pants. My parents waited in my room until I fell asleep that night and the next night I was brought to a teen psychiatric unit at a local hospital.

My experiences in that hospital are indescribably horrific, and I swear I still have nightmares of that place. Many patients were sedated or restrained in straight jackets, there were cockroaches in the bedrooms, the only contact with the outside world was through a payphone, showers were supervised, and restricted items included sweatshirt strings and shoelaces. It didn't really set in that I was in a psychiatric hospital until I was being evaluated and asked if I ever heard voices that no one else heard. By the end of the week I was officially diagnosed with major depressive disorder and put on more anti-depressants. That week in the hospital was the lowest point in my life.

I wish I could say that once I got out things turned around completely, but the truth is I was still pulling everyday, and I even cut on occasion. I was forced by the hospital to attend dialectical and cognitive behavior therapy twice a week with my parents. Believe it or not, that therapy would change my life and eventually help me stop cutting altogether. If there was one thing the hospital showed me, it's that there are so many people worse off than me. I channeled that gratitude into every step of my therapy, and it motivated me to want to get better. They screened me for something called borderline personality disorder, which I had all the criteria for but couldn't be officially diagnosed with because I was too young. Regardless, It felt oddly reassuring to know there was a reason for my sudden mood swings, extreme emotions, and chaotic relationships. Sadly, despite the numerous efforts of my therapists at the center for cognitive and dialectical behavior therapy, they were not able to help me cease pulling.

Believe me, I tried just about every tactic I could come up with to stop myself from pulling. The strategies ranged from playing with silly putty and stress balls to wearing tape on each of my fingers so I couldn't grip the hair, to putting ankle weights on my wrists so it was difficult to lift my hand to my head. I found that one of the best strategies was actually more mental than physical. What helped me the most was communicating with other people who suffered from trichotillomania. The first time I went to a workshop in NYC hosted by the Trichotillomania Learning Center I couldn't believe all the similarities between the so-called "trichsters" and myself. I thought I was the only one in the world who examined her hair follicle and sometimes chewed on it after pulling it from her head, and yet there I was in a room full of trichsters who did the exact same thing. Educating myself about trichotillomania made me want to educate others. I couldn't help but think that maybe if people understood the condition, it might help them have an easier time accepting it.

The next two years of high school were mundane and are honestly a bit of a blur to me. My struggles in school and fights with my parents became common occurrences. I continued in therapy and tried hard to smile for the sake of my relationship with my friends. I even dated a guy for a while! That ended pretty badly though when he pulled my wig off while we were hanging out because he was curious about what I looked like without it. Not only did he violate my privacy and make me extremely uncomfortable, he proclaimed "Ew, no wonder you wear the wig…keep it on!" when he saw my bald head. I continuously missed out on events in my life because I was held back by trichotillomania. I refused to go to sleepovers because I didn't want to take my wig off, I could never go to pool parties or swim at the beach despite the fact that I love the water, and I never went on rides at theme parks. Looking back I wish I had done the things I love instead of letting my lack of hair hold me back.

     I've always been a compassionate person, and strangely enough, even though I couldn't stop myself from pulling, I wanted to help other people stop. One day I decided to make a YouTube channel on a whim. I started off filming myself "vlogging" about trichotillomania and other mental illnesses on my laptop webcam. Eventually I decided to make a video in which I took off my wig and talked about my battle with trich. Never in my wildest dreams could I have imagined that the video would gain popularity on a blogging website called Tumblr and become known in the trichotillomania community. I watched in awe as the views on my channel racked up, and I received lots of messages from people confessing their hair pulling to me. To date, my YouTube channel has 13,000 views! The positive aspect of my exposure is knowing I've helped some other trichsters feel that they aren't alone in their fight. The downside was being contacted by shows like "My Strange Addiction" and "True Life" that wanted nothing more then to exploit me and make trichotillomania look bad.

     In October of 2012 I attended my second Trichotillomania Learning Center workshop in NYC. There was nothing special about this day, and I didn't plan on the changes that were about to take place in my life. I was going to simply talk with other trichsters and feel a little less alone. Christina Pearson, my role model and the founder of TLC who has been pull free for years, spoke about loving yourself and accepting who you are. After her presentation I told her about my frustrations with trich, and how badly wanted to stop, to which she responded: "It's okay if you're not ready to stop right now. Someday you will be."

     Suddenly something clicked inside of me. I swear at that very moment I became determined to change the course of my life forever. I remember telling my mom, "I don't want to wait for someday; I'm ready now." I made a promise to myself that day to try harder then ever before to stop pulling my hair. I swore I would not give in like I had all the times before. I knew that one thing holding me back was the pressure of keeping my hair pulling a secret, and so a few days later I made a post on my public Facebook page explaining that I had trichotillomania. To help people understand it I posted links to the trichotillomania learning center webpage and asked people to keep an open mind. The response I received was emotionally overwhelming. Family, friends, and peers alike showed their love and support for me. People started throwing around words like "brave" and "inspirational." That was the moment I began to love myself again. Since the Facebook post had been such a success, I decided to also give a talk about trichotillomania in front of my Christian existence class. My goal became to educate as many people as possible about the condition.

Ignorance and lack of knowledge about hair pulling is half the problem, and it's a problem that we can solve if we try hard enough. As my days "pull free" tallied higher and higher, I didn't want to break the trend. The first week or two was easy because of my high motivation but then the urges got stronger. I often compare my urge to pull in the second and third month of being "pull free" to the feeling you get when you are trying to hold your breath for a long time. The need to feel the follicle disconnect from my scalp was just as strong as the need for oxygen to fill my lungs.

Yet, against all the odds I continued to keep my hands off my head. The question I get most often from fellow trichsters is how I stopped pulling. I so desperately wish I could give an exact formula to stop or hand you a pill and say, "just take this." What I can say is that it was the hardest feat of my life thus far. I had to be conscious of where my hands were one hundred percent of the time. I counted the days "pull free " and the higher the number got, the more motivated I became. One night I got into bed and realized I hadn't felt the urge to pull all day. Slowly the urges lessened and I knew I was in control of my own actions. An important part of my recovery was realizing trichotillomania does not define who I am. I am Katherine Elizabeth Paris, the girl who loves to read, play music, and help those in need, not Katherine "the girl who pulls her hair." I had to rediscover who I was apart from my diagnosis. Somewhere down the line when others defined me by my condition, I had begun to define myself that way too.

After being six months pull free I had the privilege of not only attending the Trichotillomania Learning Center conference, but also speaking at it. I presented a workshop for teens where we talked about things that help us not pull and also discussed the things that make us unique besides trichotillomania. It was an honor to be able to present that workshop, and I met some of the most beautiful and kindhearted individuals I have ever been lucky enough to know. I also spoke on a panel of incredible individuals who all had success stories involving trichotillomania or skin picking disorder. Some, like me, had stopped their pulling cold turkey. Others had learned to love themselves and accept who they are despite their struggles with hair pulling or skin picking. The women I spoke with on that panel gave me the inspiration I needed to continue being pull free even when life got stressful.

I am ecstatic to report that as I sit here typing out my story I am a year and two months pull free. I am blessed that my hair has grown back full and thick! Recently I was able to put my hair into a ponytail for the first time. I cried when I realized that was the first time I had put my hair back in over five years. My entire life turned around and now it's hard to remember a time when I couldn't picture my future. Not only did I graduate high school with a full head of hair, but also got into my first choice college where I now study psychology in hopes of someday becoming a psychologist who specializes in treating those suffering from trich.

After kicking trichotillomania's ass I decided I had enough determination to do anything I want in life. So I began changing my life in other ways as well, such as losing over one hundred pounds in less than a year. Being a somewhat religious person, I believe that I was given trichotillomania for a reason. Even more strongly, I believe I was given the strength to overcome the condition for a reason. I know with ever fiber of my being that I am meant to help those who still feel alone and alienated because of their hair pulling. I wish I could talk to every single person still suffering from trich and tell them that they are precious, and they are worth it.

Everyone has a struggle and everyone has a story. It's imperative to remember that before judging a person, and I hope society can start realizing that. If there is one thing I want people to take away from my story, it is that anything is possible. I can promise that the journey to being pull free won't be a walk in the park, but it is so worth it. And if you don't want to be pull free, don't beat yourself up about it. Remember to be gentle with yourself and love every aspect of who you are.

To wrap up my story I'll leave you with this: despite all the pain and strife trichotillomania caused me, I wouldn't erase it from my life even if I could. My obstacles and battles have made me the strong individual I am today. I believe those with trichotillomania are the most beautiful, compassionate, creative people, and someday we will change the world for the better.

*I can be found on Twitter: @katparis.

2
FINDING PEACE
HOPE, MID-THIRTIES, UK

In 1979 Margaret Thatcher began her political rule in the UK. The Yorkshire Ripper was also still at large. I guess you might say that it was a landmark year. However, amongst these goings-on, I know without a shadow of doubt, that the main focus for my parents that year was my arrival. In the spring of 1979, I was born in a small working class village in the UK. My name is Hope.

I am the younger of two daughters. Various pets including dogs, cats, rabbits, and birds increased our family numbers and added a real touch of warmth to our home. Whilst money was not easy for my parents living in a council house (a form of public housing in the UK), we always had food on our plate, toys to play with, and infinite cuddles on tap. I was, and still am, a very affectionate girl, and I know this is due to the love that filled my family home.

I have memories of sitting on my mum's knee and falling asleep against her tummy. One of my favourite things was to wake up in the morning and run to my parents' bedroom, where my mum would pretend to be asleep as I climbed in beside her and whispered, "Are you awake yet?"

Mum would try to catch a few more minutes by keeping her eyes

21

shut and pretending she couldn't hear me, whilst my dad was downstairs building the coal fire and preparing breakfast. But Mum would always give in and scoop me into her arms.

My dad has always been a real hands-on dad, and he always spent a lot of time with my sister and I. My biggest childhood memories of my dad are of him arriving home from work in the early evening. Sometimes I would hide under our living room sideboard and make him find me on his arrival home. I barked and pretended to be our pet dog, and he would act surprised when he opened the sideboard door to find me crouched and giggling inside.

I was and continue to be a sensitive girl, and my earliest memory of this is when I was on a family walk in the countryside at the age of four. One of the most exciting parts of the four mile walk was an iron bridge that we crossed over whilst the river flowed smoothly yet powerfully underneath. I recall crossing the bridge one day and looking down at the water beneath, where I saw a baby doll floating down the river. I burst into tears and begged my dad to go down and rescue the doll, not because I wanted her for myself, but because I was genuinely heartbroken that this little doll was floating away without a little girl to love and care for her. My mother pacified me by telling me that the river would flow out into the sea, and that the doll would be washed up on a beach to be found by a little girl who would love her.

At school, I really liked art, and I would bring home all kinds of art projects from school. Looking back, they ranged from the fantastic to the positively ghastly. Many of them were nothing more than blobs of paint on a piece of paper, whilst others were really quite good and beyond that of a young child. I remember making a cardboard teddy bear whose legs moved when you pulled a piece of string. My parents pinned my artwork above their bed and my mum called it "her gallery." I came home from school regularly with my latest offering, and it gave me so much pleasure to see that my artwork made them happy.

I guess you could say that family life was pretty much perfect, and I was a sensitive, yet happy, little girl.

I don't know what happened to me at the tender age of six. I had no life-changing events, nor did I have any behavioural problems. However, at this young age, I very suddenly started to pull out my eyelashes. I don't remember the first time I pulled. All I know is that one day when I was standing in my aunt and uncle's house, my uncle made a comment about my lack of eyelashes, and my dad replied rather sharply, saying that they had told me not to do it. I just remember standing there, in the hallway, knowing that they were right: I didn't have any eyelashes. I knew I had pulled them out, but I had no idea what was wrong with this. It just felt like second nature, like breathing.

The earlier years of my pulling are rather hazy, but I do remember becoming more and more secretive about it as I realised that I was engaging in something that was not desirable to others. Around about the age of six or seven, I recall being taken to the doctor (the doctor who had known me since I was born) to find out why I was doing this. As she looked at me over her glasses whilst my dad told her I was plucking out my eyelashes, I just couldn't see what the big deal was. Why was everyone angry with me? I liked pulling out my lashes…what was the problem?

Mum and Dad discussed my doctor's visit over the dinner table that evening, and I sat in silence wishing that the conversation would just go away. Even at that age, it pained me to see that I was making my parents angry. Another day around about this time, Miss Montgomery (my primary 2 teacher) chastised me in front of my entire school class when she saw me touching my eyelashes and said something to the effect of it being "gross" or "disgusting."

I wasn't really sure what was so disgusting about the behaviour that just felt so natural and good to me. To be honest, I am not even sure I would have realised I was touching my eyelashes had she not pointed it out. But I felt bad and somewhat ashamed. My primary 3 teacher also used my bald eyelids as an example of the word "eyelashes" in class one day when we were learning new words. Although I was only seven, I was mortified. I'm not really sure what happened in these early stages of my pulling, but the next few years that ensued were to become the saddest of my childhood.

I don't remember the first time I was bent over my parents' bed and smacked on my bottom as a punishment for pulling out my eyelashes; it happened far too often. I know that I wasn't a bad child (at times I wish I had acted up more often; I was almost too good), so the majority of my punishments were the result of being caught after pulling my eyelashes and not for being generally naughty. Regularly, my parents did make attempts to reward me when I didn't pull (for example star-charts), but they would get frustrated and upset when the star-charts hung starless on the wall and the punishments would start again. Another walk to the bedroom, another punishment bent over the bed. More tears as I cried alone in my room after it was over.

I developed a genuine fear of being caught for pulling. I felt truly unable to control these urges to pull out my eyelashes, but I was terrified of gaps in my lashes being seen. Sometimes Mum would come to the bathroom and count how many eyelashes I had on my eyelids and she would tell me that she would be checking to see if any more went missing. One time, I was given a deadline: "you've got two weeks and I want to see progress," she said in a firm tone. Deep down, I knew that I would have to work a miracle to survive two weeks without pulling any more lashes.

As the days passed, I was able to get away with losing one or two that went unnoticed, and I felt so relieved when Mum would count the eyelashes and not notice that I had pulled. The smile on her face made me happy, and I felt I didn't have to hide. So as the two weeks developed, I would continue to "try to get away with" pulling a few a day. One day, I was at my nearby grandmother's house with my mum when they started to talk about my eyelash pulling. My mum said, "I'm very proud of Hope, she has not been pulling, I have been checking. Come over and look at her eyes." As my Gran came over to look, I remember sitting in the chair believing in my heart, "She didn't notice yesterday, nor the day before, so she won't today." As I sat and smiled waiting for my compliment, my mum's voice just turned to stone, and I realised that I had failed in my mission to hide my eyelash loss. She ordered me to walk back down to my house and wait for dad, who would be "seeing" me when he got home from work. I was not only breaking everyone else's hearts but also my own. And so life continued like this between the ages of six through ten. A loving childhood with periods of sadness dotted in between.

In the March of 1988 when I was nine years old, I had somehow managed to grow in my eyelashes and went to school one morning like any other little girl. I remember it was a Wednesday. I was in gym class that afternoon, and I had an overwhelming urge to pull, so I did. I pulled out every single eyelash from my top eyelids during gym class and then felt an immense sense of panic as we were dismissed. I ran to the girls' toilets on my way back to the classroom and looked in the mirror, desperately hoping that I had not done any noticeable damage. Instead, what stared back at me was one single eyelash, right in the centre of my left eyelid. Every single other lash on my top eyelid was gone. The single eyelash looked stupid, so I took my little fingers and pulled it out. It was done.

I was afraid to go home that day, and the 10-15 minute walk home after school to my house, seemed to last forever. As I approached my back door, I looked through the windows of the door and saw my mum standing in the kitchen, pottering around. Dad wasn't home from work yet. I decided to try to hide the damage I had done by pretending to be a monster, so I took off my wine coloured red coat, put the hood over my face, and came in the door walking like a zombie with my face covered. Mum laughed and said, "Oh here's a monster!" For a few short moments, I felt relieved, before I ran upstairs to my room to play (and hide). About ten minutes later, mum called me from the kitchen to ask if I would run to the local shop to pick up a few things for dinner, so I ran down the stairs and stood in the kitchen whilst she took out her purse to give me the money.

I'll never forget what happened next. Mum suddenly dropped her head in her hands on the kitchen unit, crying, "Oh no, oh no, not again, on no…" I knew I had been caught. She dropped her purse and took me upstairs to my bedroom where she grabbed me by my arm and just shook me violently, shouting, "Why, why," as she struggled to contain her composure. Mum was absolutely hysterical and seemed to have lost all control. As I cried and tried to explain that I just didn't know why I had done it, I looked out of my bedroom window and saw my best friend walking down garden path, obviously coming to invite me out to play. As my friend knocked on our house door, my mum told me to stay where I was whilst she went downstairs and answered the door.

"Hope isn't coming out to play, she has been a very bad girl."

My mum came back upstairs and dragged me from my bedroom into her bedroom, but instead of hitting me, she went to the bedroom wall where my art gallery was displayed and started to tear all of my artwork off the wall. As the pieces of childish artwork hit the bedroom floor, I picked up the cardboard teddy bear, whose legs moved when you pulled on the string. I offered the bear back to my mum, but she cried loudly and shouted, "It just reminds me of what you've done!"

I felt heartbroken, but most of all, I felt like I had broken my mother's heart. My mum took me downstairs, opened the back door, and told me, "Go to the garden shed, this house is too good for you!" So, whilst dinner was cooking and whilst waiting for my dad to come home, I went outside into the garden and stood alone, as mum closed the back door of the house and went inside.

I didn't want to go into the garden shed. The garden shed was sometimes fun to play in. But not today. I wanted to be in my house, with my mum, dad and sister, enjoying a family dinner and cuddling up afterwards as we usually did. But I knew I had been bad, that she was very angry, and that the house wasn't an option. So instead of going into the garden shed to wait for dinner, I defiantly continued up the garden path, opened the garden gate, and went for a short walk down the residential street where I lived. I stared at the concrete, crying, waiting on the punishment that would ensue when my dad was home from work. I have no idea how much time passed out there on the street, but my mum calling me home for dinner finally interrupted my thoughts. As I approached the house, I hoped in my heart that she would be happy to see me, but instead I was met with: "I told you to go to the garden shed!"

Dinner was silent that evening, the usual procedure followed, and then I spent the rest of the time in my bedroom alone. My heart was broken. Even though I was only nine, I was able to see that this was the worst that had ever happened, and I knew this would not pass. That happened on a Wednesday.

Mum still wasn't speaking to me on Thursday morning, but she did put a letter in my hands as I left for school.

"Give that to your teacher," she said and walked away.

She could not look me in the eye, and there was no kiss goodbye as I went to school, no nothing. I knew in my heart what this letter contained, and I didn't want my teacher to read about what I had done. So quietly in the classroom whilst no one was looking, I opened the sealed letter that was not addressed to me, and read it. It was a report of what I had done, and it asked the teacher to watch me. I felt such shame that I crumpled the letter up in my little hands, hoping that no one would ever read the contents of what had happened just a day earlier. I made the fatal error of leaving my school bag in the living room that night when I came home, before going to my room to be alone. Not much longer on that Thursday evening, I was summoned downstairs to be met by my mum, who held the opened letter in her hands.

Friday morning came and mum went with me to school and talked to my teacher about the events of the last two days. My teacher took me into her cupboard and although I can't remember what she said exactly (and I did get into trouble for opening mail not addressed to me), she gave me a cuddle, and I knew that in her eyes, everything was going to be alright. By Friday night, mum still wasn't talking to me.

My big sister took my aside and told me that I had to go and tell mum and dad how sorry I was for what I had done. I don't believe for one moment that my sister thought I was bad, but I believe that her teenage years had made her a little wiser and that she thought that the offer of an apology might break the tension in our home. I offered the apology then went back to my room, only to be called back downstairs by my mum who just wrapped her arms around me. Finally, the tension passed and we were a family again.

During those days that passed, I remember praying to God to punish me for what I had done. When I fell off my bicycle two weeks later and fractured my wrist, it all seemed quite acceptable. Looking back now, I can see the patterns of self-punishment and shame that were developing and I would take with me into my adulthood.

A few weeks later, my parents took me to the general practitioner again where I was referred to a psychiatrist. That day of my first assessment, the psychiatrist told my parents that punishment was not the right thing. Mum and Dad emerged from the room and said "We're not going to punish you anymore darling, we are going see what can be done." The psychiatrist could not give a name for what I was doing to myself, but finally, I was free. As the years passed between 10-16 years old, I bounced between psychiatrists, psychologists and behaviour therapists, none of whom really understood this behaviour that I was presenting, but this was life as I moved into puberty in the late 1980s into the early 1990s. Although I had not stopped pulling, my parents were at peace with it, though school children might point and laugh. But I had my parents and it meant the world. And I know that they only did what they did because they didn't understand.

***

My teenage years were lonely, and I expressed myself by composing music on my electric piano and listening to a lot of "dark" songs. Looking back, I firmly believe that I had clinical depression around my mid-teenage years. I had this "thing," still nameless, that I desperately tried to hide from the world. This thing that no one else had, and this thing that completely defined how I felt about my physical appearance, my self-worth, and fundamentally, myself. I went through rigorous make-up processes as I grew older, learning how to hide, what I believed, was a disfigurement. For that reason, I never had the boyfriends (real or pretend) that most girls had at high school, nor did I ever dare to talk to a boy I liked, because I believed I would be rejected on the basis of my physical appearance.

I had a few light dalliances with boys but it wasn't until the age of 23 that I met Kevin, who was 3 years younger than me, and like me, had never had a serious partner before. After months of being friends, we took the step to enter into what was the first real relationship for both of us. I felt safe with Kevin, but I was terrified that he would one day notice the secret on my face. Kevin and I were not in a physically intimate relationship, so that meant that we spent a lot of time generally hanging out as best friends. When watching movies, I would be sure to tilt my head at the angle that would conceal my false eyelashes the most. When cuddling on the sofa, I would tuck my head into his chest so that my eyes were not in close direct eye line with his. I was hiding from my boyfriend.

It was not until May of 2002 that I discovered a name for pulling. I was crying one night at the home computer after another failed attempt at not pulling. By now, I was also pulling from the temporal areas of my scalp, my eyebrows were thinning out, and my pubic area was (and still is) mildly scarred from digging out ingrown hairs. My trich was severe, and it was spreading. I typed "pulling out eyelashes" into the search engine and could not believe my eyes when this word popped up on every hit:

Trichotillomania

Trichotillomania

Trichotillomania

Trichotillomania

Trichotillomania

Tricho-tillo-what? There was a name for this monster inside me? And more importantly, was it even the slightest bit possible that I was not alone with this? I sat for hours that evening scrolling through the pages of the Internet and finally came across a page based in the USA with contact email addresses of ladies I could email. I randomly chose to email "Dori" and sat down and typed my first ever email about this. I wrote about the things I did to myself; how it felt; how it made me feel; how it broke my heart. I needed to know if I had this condition. When Dori replied (from Texas) within 24 hours, my heart skipped so many beats. It was like I had wings and I suddenly believed I could fly. I had found a friend, and via Dori, I found Camille, Lindy, Doreen and Jennifer and correspondence between the UK and USA was frequent.

The breakthrough of this finding encouraged me to tell my parents that I finally had a name for my pulling. They were taken aback and Mum spent an evening reading about it on the Internet. I even told Kevin (albeit, I told him in tears for fear of him freaking out and leaving me) and he accepted it and wrapped his arms around me. As time went on, I became brave enough to let him see me without my camouflage. I began what was to become ten months completely pull-free. This was the first time I had been completely pull-free, and I felt beautiful and normal. I could accept myself, and Kevin went through this journey with me. The pull-freedom passed and I relapsed, but I always treasure the year of 2002.

However, something was not right with my heart, and although I was entering a new chapter of my life, I was not at peace with the events of my childhood. I now knew that I had a severe case of a diagnosed condition and as I thought about the shame and punishment that my parents poured upon me, I felt anger stirring. How could they? I was just a child who nature had chosen as a candidate for trichotillomania. I spoke with Kevin one night and told him everything, and he comforted me as he listened to the events of my childhood. As I spoke, I felt anger increasing in my soul (anger was not an emotion I was used to feeling) and we agreed together that I had to tell my parents how much they had hurt me. So on the 22nd of December, unable to tell them face-to-face, I wrote an email to my mum and dad, and then went to Kevin's house. I returned on the 23rd of December 2002, hoping to receive a warm hug and some sort of apology, but instead, my mum was in pieces as she told me that I would never know how hard it was for them and that they would never apologise for what happened, because they did their best. Again, there was tension and we barely spoke on the lead up to Christmas day. On Christmas morning, my mum cried in the bathroom after we opened our Christmas presents, and I could no longer handle the silence, so I packed my things and moved in with Kevin and his parents.

It was when I didn't return home after three days that I finally got a text from my mum asking me to come home to talk to her and my dad. Kevin came with me, and they sat me down and told me that they missed me and wanted me to come home, but that they didn't think it was right to say sorry for those years of my childhood. My dad told me how in his childhood days, it was normal to "get a boot in the backside" if he was naughty, and my mum agreed that as I had no children, I wasn't in any place to judge parenting. So as we talked, we agreed to let this pass, and it was swept under the carpet and things slowly returned to normal.

The years passed, and as I moved through my twenties, I completed my master's degree in psychology. I was not at peace with my trichotillomania but was learning to hide it relatively well and live with it. I still felt like an unattractive girl with issues and was often taunted by memories from the past, so I went to therapy to deal with the anger and self-esteem issues, and I believe that I worked through them well. My therapist and I reached a place where we worked on acceptance instead of recovery, as my trichotillomania was now in its twenty-somethingth year and I could not imagine my life without pulling in it.

Life came and went, boyfriends changed, friends changed, but one thing that remained was my passion for psychology. I found my voice and became more confident and outgoing, and in my mid to late twenties, I finally blossomed into the girl that had been hiding for too many years. I started my Ph.D (researching trichotillomania) and through this, I was able to go to the 2011 TLC conference in San Francisco where I met hundreds of people just like me, whilst investing in the research side of the condition. There (and again at the 2013 conference in New Jersey) I met new friends. I also met up with people I had been talking to on online support groups, like Christina, Nathan, Elizabeth, Lindsay and Heather.

Meeting fellow trichsters is like meeting people who are in the same club as you. It's not the coolest club, but you're in it together and you don't have to do much to break the ice. To this day, I'm still in touch with the people I met there.

Before I left San Francisco, I bought Cheryn Salazar's book, *You Are Not Alone* and on returning home, I took it to my parents' house. I had not yet read the book but gave it to Mum and Dad to read as they were really interested to learn more and were so proud of everything I had achieved so far. If only I had read that book before I gave it to them. I was having drinks with my friends one Friday evening when I received a text message from Mum:

"Just finished Cheryn Salazar's excellent book. I want to apologise for my ignorance all those years ago and the hurt I caused you. Please take this as a sincere apology to my darling Hope, XXX."

What had been in that book? What had my mum read? I collected the book and took it on vacation with me to the Spanish island of Tenerife, and as I sat on a terrace with a cool beer reading it, I arrived at a chapter specifically addressed to parents. The chapter repeated many times how important it is to stand by a child with trichotillomania, and never let the child endure shame for what they are unable to handle. I almost broke at what I had given my mother to read, and had I known, I believe I would not have given it to her. I sent my mum a text message from Spain and told her that I was so sorry for what she had read about, and she replied saying that it was insightful, and that they love me and were so proud of me.

I found peace.

***

I'm now 34 and I still feel stirring emotions when I see photos of myself as a child with bald eyelids. I can't explain what the emotion is that I feel. When I see that young child, and other young children with trichotillomania, what I feel is a genuine sadness but a real drive to reach out and help. I have made it my mission to raise and spread awareness about trichotillomania.

Every year in my job, I stand in front of 600 young adults and educate them on what trichotillomania is, how it can affect one, and how people can try to understand it. I have not revealed my trichotillomania to most of my colleagues and friends as I still have a deep rooted shame of it, but I have revealed my passion for researching in this area. Working in trichotillomania research has allowed me the chance to offer students assistant work, and every year I have students lining up to help out because the area fascinates them. So far, seven students have worked on trichotillomania research with me. Some of them could be the future of our psychology research, and it makes me proud to see them find a passion in this area.

I strive to introduce my research students to trichsters, to whom they can ask questions and learn the most they can. Marion (a trichster) travelled from London to see me and sat for three hours over dinner whilst three of my research students asked her about her 40 years of pulling. Bryony came from Edinburgh and had a coffee with another of my research students, after which they ended up swapping email addresses to share resources.

My mission is to educate and raise awareness, to reach out to others struggling in shame and isolation. Although, behind the thick eyeliner and false eyelashes, I am still hiding, I am getting the word out in the UK, and I have found that many people want to know more about it (and often know someone who does it). As the work develops, I have been able to meet the parents of children who pull out their hair and it's the children who hold a special place in my heart. I never want them to feel the isolation I did. I went to a soft play area once to chat to Carrie, the mother of Alana (who is currently in recovery) as she played nearby. John from California, who attended a TLC conference with his teenage daughter Marie, impressed me. Marie and I wrapped our arms around each other on the final day of the 2011 conference and I wept in her arms as the children on the stage talked about their recovery. I felt so proud to hold her in my arms, watching this young girl moving into adulthood, taking these brave steps, shepherded by her father.

So, what have I learned? I've learned that it's possible to live with trichotillomania, and that although there will be days I will cry, that it doesn't define me. Things might be hard, and it can be a long and tough road, but the only way is up. I've learned that if we all work together (trichsters, parents, researchers), that we can move mountains. I've learned that some people just don't know any better and that it's our job to educate them. Finally, I've learned that I am stronger and happier than I ever believed I could be.

***

This is dedicated to my mum, dad, sister, and Kevin. Without them, this journey would not have been possible. Thank you for loving me unconditionally.

I also want to thank the trichotillomania community for the love and daily support that we share. All things are possible.

3
YOU HAVE TRICH. IT DOESN'T HAVE YOU.
BILLY, THIRTIES, NEW YORK

What did I just do? I asked myself. I sat there, a puzzled look on my face. To this day I can't explain why it happened. Thirty years later and I don't know why I started pulling out my hair. Maybe I will never know. But the journey has had its ups and downs.

The first time I pulled from my scalp was in the spring of 1985. I was sitting in my second grade classroom finishing up a lesson and clearing off my desk. As I sat patiently waiting for the next assignment to start, I scratched my head. About ten seconds later I pulled a hair out of my scalp and observed it for a few seconds.

I noticed the thickness of the tip. The root was nice and healthy and felt incredibly good to me. I dropped the hair on the floor and about 15 minutes later did it again. This time my curiosity about the root grew even more. I gently placed the tip of my hair on my lips and the sensation was like nothing I have felt since.

I rubbed it across my lips and chewed and the bulb. The chewing of the bulb really excited me. Not in a sexual way, but like a bizarre adrenaline rush. I went home and told my mother what I did. She just told me never to do it again. I tried to stop, but my first of many bald spots appeared about two weeks later.

I was mortified by it. My mother was able to cover it so it was not noticeable. When asked why I did it I said it was because my teacher (that had a great fondness for me) was leaving to take another position. I felt I had to give a somewhat rational excuse for the strange behavior. Can you imagine a 7 year old having to think up lies so they do not sound crazy?

I stopped pulling for about a year and a half. In fall of 1986 my hair pulling returned with pretty horrible results. It became a non-stop habit as I pulled, chewed, and left clumps of hair behind me like some sick Hansel and Gretel.

The bald spots became harder to cover. My mother tried everything to help me cover them. Most mornings we spent about 45 minutes shading the spots in with an eyebrow pencil. Between the pulling and the coloring my scalp took an absolute beating.

Therapy was the next step. After therapy came medication, and then after therapy a couple of hospitalizations, because trich brought his friends anxiety and depression. The meds never really worked for me. I would stop for a bit, but the side effects were usually pretty shitty. When I turned 20 I made the decision to stop taking my meds. I could not handle being tired anymore, not to mention the other laundry list of issues that came with them.

For the first 25 years of my life I never came across one other person with trich. It was just me, always feeling as though I had one strike against me. All of that changed when I connected to the Internet. I found TLC and others that fight the same battle. I was relieved to realize I was not alone.

I have been pulling for so long I doubt I will ever be pull free. I have become ok with that. Helping others with trich has helped me a great deal. About four years ago I realized I wanted to make some noise for my disorder. I figured if I can't beat it, I could at least help spread awareness and make those that are hurting feel a little better.

I had been doing stand-up comedy for about two years when it dawned on me. A comedy benefit for trich would be amazing. I joined a trich facebook group and posted my idea. The response was amazing. In fact, it was so amazing that I started a trich podcast.

The podcast leading up to the benefit was surreal. Every Tuesday night at 11 pm about 75 hair pullers would listen, call in, or hang out in the cast chat room just for trich talk. It was so great to have a little community just for us. I didn't focus on curing trich or trying to stop. I wanted those tuning in to just be comfortable complaining about it. The stigma for this disorder is harsh.

It was an important message for me to convey to the listeners that forgiving yourself should be *numero uno* on your list. Follow forgiveness with a strong support group. I know it's hard, but if you find genuine people that do not judge you it makes your journey less bumpy. Those that understand are amazing.

I started getting emails from other pullers from around the world. China, Germany, and Saudi Arabia. It was such a great feeling. Years ago I thought I was the only one of my kind, then all of a sudden I am talking about trichophagia to someone on the other side of the world.

All the emails and phone calls had one thing in common; they all had overtones of shame. When replying to the emails I tried to instill feelings of self-worth and encouraged acceptance of the hair pulling. Reading all the emails and listening to all the stories on the podcast really helped me with my own thoughts about trich.

I remember growing up and feeling such animosity toward myself for pulling my hair. I was my own harshest critic. But in speaking with everyone and being able to show them life wasn't all so bleak, my own eyes were opened and I could start to forgive myself. I had to practice what I preached. To this day I still get emails and tweets from hair pullers thanking me for showing them a different way of coping instead of just trying to be "pull free."

When it came time for the comedy benefit for TLC I was unbelievably nervous. I had done so much preparation and so much work I wanted it to be perfect. And it was. About 50 hair pullers from the New York area and even a handful that had travelled packed New York Comedy Club to just about standing room only capacity.

I could not believe it. After decades of living with embarrassment, lying to people about how I got my bald spots, therapists, medication and hospitalizations I was actually proud of my hair pulling. I was able to take something that had for a long time been a negative in my life and turn it into a positive.

So many helped get the benefit off the ground that night. I had people from all over the country helping. Someone from Pennsylvania helped with video, and I found comedians that had trich. Their willingness to come "out the closet" and appear on the show was incredible.

Sharing a stage with others that suffered as I did was cathartic. Realizing that people walked in the same shoes as I did and used the same methods of coping was really terrific. For once I was in control and had an amount of acceptance I never had before.

My gratitude for everyone involved that night can never be measured. For one night I was looked upon with different eyes. I wasn't the guy that pulled out all his hair. I was someone with a message and just wanted to get it out there. And I accomplished that.

About a year and a half after the benefit I got to have another incredible moment thanks to trich. In January of 2011, I was interviewed by Howard Stern about my trich. Talking to one of the most famous men in radio history about my wacky affliction was a surreal moment. He was more than gracious and understanding. After talking to Howard I noticed the stigma of trich seeming to fade a little.

In the past year we had a Miss America hopeful "come out," as well as an actress. There have also been characters in television and movies portrayed with trich. Who would have thought? Maybe it is our turn to have a little spotlight. Society seems far more forgiving then it was 15 or 20 years ago. It would be great to just be able to live with it and have others understand, instead of having to explain it, let alone get someone to pronounce trichotillomania.

It took a long time, but I am no longer the guy that pulls out his hair. I am Billy, and I happen to have a rare disorder. I have realized what I can accomplish for others like me and myself in the past few years. I hope to help by being a voice for those who have not found their own yet. For those of you struggling at the moment, remember you have trich. It does not have you.

Live your life and don't despair. There are amazing moments to be had, and when you have them, you realize it is all worth it.

My biggest fear today comes in the form of a 30 pound little boy. I had long said I would not wish trich on my worst enemy. Now I have some fear that my son Jake will start doing it. As I stated earlier I pull in front of just about anyone now. I know he sees me doing it. And it is through his eyes that I see I need to stop.

I sometimes wonder where I would be right now if I took a more serious approach to my recovery. I have pretty much taken all of my advice from all my therapists with a grain of salt. In my mind getting advice for someone that hasn't lived through it is difficult. No behavior modification has worked and the meds were a crap shoot. It has to come from inside me. I was given this disorder for some odd reason. Every day is a battle. Every day I am stronger for it. Now I see the forest through the trees. I have to keep myself under control, not just for me, but for Jake too. I am sure I will have to explain it to him eventually.

When that time comes I don't want my story to be a tale of bad medication and getting teased. I hope it will be a story filled with pretty bad ass moments, like headlining and selling out a comedy club in New York City, being interviewed by Howard Stern, or just staying up late and exchanging emails with someone that is having a rough time. Giving myself to others is the best way to get rid of the horrible feelings that come along with this disorder.

My wife and son have provided me a comfort level with myself I never thought I would have. I don't need to hide, although I should. My wife is constantly telling me to stop pulling at my beard. I know I need to stop, and now it has to happen more than ever.

Last October I came down with a horrible staph infection on the right side of my neck. I was diagnosed with MRSA, which is a penicillin resistant kind of bacterial infection. It is extremely contagious and if not treated properly can be dangerous even fatal. MRSA attacks through skin vibrations like cuts, abbreviations, or another kind of skin issue. Now pulling for me has also become dangerous.

I still pull, and though I have not been infected again, it is a crappy experience. My son and the MRSA are signs to me that I need to stop, but I am not sure how. I know meds and therapy aren't the way to go for me. I need to find my own way, and with all that has happened in the past few years I have the confidence that I will.

I love my wife and my son and I am forever grateful to those that have been able to see past my issues and to see who I am and what I am about. Thirty years of this has been a crazy ride but looking back I have no regrets.

In closing I want everyone out there reading this to try something. Log on to Facebook and start talking to others with trich. Try starting an online support group or a group in your community. Don't live in shame. Own your life and strut your great qualities.

You get to see what people are really made of when you live with this bonkers disorder. Those that accept you are by your side no matter what. The others are not worthy of your time or your uniqueness.

We can see past the b.s. that most people can't. We can sense what others can't. We also feel more. These are all great, yet harrowing qualities. It takes tremendous trial and error in order to cope with society. But it makes you smarter, stronger, and more in tune with yourself.

When you pull, forgive yourself. Don't let a slip-up negate you as a person. You didn't ask for this, yet it is your burden, and I feel for each and every one of you. But do not despair. You already know those that support you.

You already know your worth. Don't be bogged down by others' perception of you. Always be the better person, even if it hurts. Make sure you are surrounded by peace and love. You have enough baggage without hooking anyone else's trailer up to your tractor.

Be the best hair puller you can. It is all going to be ok. Pulling is not the end of the world. Living in seclusion is no way to go through life. Even with some of my cool experiences there is plenty I missed. I do not have any regrets, but every now and then I think of what I could have done differently.

The fact we wake up in the morning is already a win. In the grand scheme of things we were always on the outside looking in. That used to bother me to no end. Then I just decided to enjoy the outside.

4

DEFINED BY LOVE
DEBI, THIRTIES, NEW YORK

I'm a creature of habit. I eat the same foods every day. I sit on the same spot on the couch. Routine, order, and predictability are the cornerstones of my life. It's all about comfort. Ever since I was a child, I've been anxious and sensitive and feeling as though I have control in my life is very important. Around age 10, I developed a coping mechanism where I would pull my hair to help myself feel better and in control (when in reality my behavior was out of control). However, it wasn't until years later that I realized the reasons why I actually pulled.

Recalling memories from childhood is a strange thing. Certain events stick with you, but the farther you get away from that event the less accurate your recollection becomes. The earliest memory I have of pulling my hair is sitting at my desk in fifth grade and noticing white flakes of dandruff against the dark wood of my desk. Somehow I pulled an eyebrow and began moving the dandruff around with the hair. It feels almost morbid and gross to write it down, but I was in elementary school and children do strange things every day. It's odd how we all start out with a lack of shame about our behavior but quickly learn that what we do is not accepted or desired behavior, and we must learn to fall back into society's box of rules that's been established for all to follow.

I have no clue if anyone saw me pushing around my dandruff that day in school. Had I been aware of my surroundings and not so focused on this strange new pulling sensation, I wonder if I would have questioned my behavior and stopped. However, it took a very long time to be conscious of what happens when I pull—or "the fall out," for a lack of a better term.

When I was in college, I lived with my brother, Greg, in a small apartment. One day he asked me why there was hair on the wall. I had no clue what he was talking about, but when I checked the situation out I realized that when I plucked my eyebrows next to the wall mirror, I'd left the hairs sticking to the wall. I was mortified! Proof of my pulling, my "bad habit," which I ignored, denied, and never wanted to discuss was now on display. I was disgusted with myself for not realizing that this is where my hair went when I pulled. After cleaning the wall, I never said anything to my brother again until a year or two later when I decided to come clean in a seven page letter to my immediate family. Not that they didn't know…

My family always knew I had trichotillomania. My parents noticed almost immediately that I was missing hair from my lashes and brows. The first step was bringing me to a counselor. Looking back, I remember feeling as though I was in a movie when the director pans out and you see a car driving up a long driveway to a big fancy building. It was in one of the nicer areas on Long Island, New York. But this didn't matter to me. I was terrified.

The first counselor we met with tried to talk to me. I don't remember anything about that session except that I had no clue what to say, because I didn't know why I was doing this to myself. So after not getting much information out of me, the counselor decided it was a family problem and brought our entire family in for the next session. My entire family consisted of my parents, my four older teenage brothers (some who often made fun of me) and my younger sister.

It was the summer between fifth and sixth grade, and I was so scared of going to the counselor that I stayed at the neighborhood pool longer than I was supposed to so I could avoid having to go. Then I cried all the way to the counselor's office and my oldest brother, Christopher, the protective one, yelled at my parents for forcing me to go. The session was unproductive in my 10 year old eyes. I cried and a few of my brothers made excuses for why they made fun of me. We never addressed why I pulled. But I'm sure it was apparent to the counselor that my household was chaotic. We never returned.

I didn't go back to a therapist until almost 20 years later. It was then that I realized that as a child, living in a chaotic home with five other siblings, many who demanded more attention that I did, I took on the conflict of the household. I absorbed it all, wanting it to be fixed. I was sensitive to everything that was going on, my brothers fighting, my parents fighting, being made fun of, feeling like I had no friends, feeling ignored. All of that created a heightened level of anxiety in me, which has become my normal way of living my life to this day. That's where my desire to control every situation originated.

I spent most of my teen years in my bedroom, reading, writing, listening to music, and all the while continuing to pull. I would go off into trances, so enthralled by the feeling of the kinky hair on my scalp, the "imperfect" lash, that I would just keep pulling until it felt "right," which never actually happened. By the time I stopped, I would have a cramp in my hand and feel utterly defeated because I knew I looked better with more hair than less.

Around age 14, I began wearing eyeliner to cover up my lack of lashes. In some ways it was good because I didn't feel as exposed, but in other ways it was worse. Then I would have black under my nails from pulling and would have to hide my hands until I washed them. Eventually I realized I was hiding a lot—my face, my hands, and my true self. Also during my teen years I had developed a small bald spot on my crown and began wearing bandanas during the summer and half ponytails during the school year to cover up my damage. My pulling areas have shifted over the years, but my lashes have always been my worst pulling area.

My ability to accept my hair pulling has been a journey over the past 20 plus years. There have been lots of baby steps. I didn't even know hair pulling had a name until I was 19 when I looked it up on the Internet and then also saw it written about in the book, *The Boy Who Couldn't Stop Washing*. At that time I was dating my now husband. I told him about my disorder, and he continued to accept me for who I was. We didn't talk about it much after I came clean, but I liked it that way. This was something I had to deal with on my own. Then I wrote the long, seven page letter to my family around age 21. Writing that letter was more for my benefit than my family's. It was my way of allowing myself to feel everything I had pushed down inside since I started pulling. It also allowed me to tell myself, *this is who I am, and it's ok*. I began the healing process and began to see myself as someone other than the girl with no lashes.

In the spring of 2004 I wrote a letter to the editor of the local Syracuse, NY newspaper to be published around National Trichotillomania Awareness Day (June 22nd). The purpose of the letter was to let other hair pullers know that they are not alone, they are not "freaks," and there is help out there for them in the form of the Trichotillomania Learning Center. A few days later, I received a call from the newspaper's health news writer. She wanted to interview me for the newspaper.

At that point I realized that if I was going to be open about my struggle, I might as well jump in with both feet. If I was willing to sign my name to a letter, I should be willing to be interviewed. We spoke on the phone for about twenty minutes and then a week or so later, they sent a photographer over to my apartment to take my picture. Now it was getting real! My story was going in the newspaper. The train was moving and there was no stopping it.

I vividly remember the day the article was published. I walked into work knowing that we had the paper delivered every day and people often read it on their lunch break. But I was hoping no one would notice the article since it was going to be in the health section. It took a little while, but finally one of my co-workers said something to me. She was very supportive and said she had heard of trichotillomania in a medical billing class. So far, so good!

Next the vice president of the company, who I worked closely with, called me into his office and mentioned the article. He said he had no clue that I had this issue and wanted to know if there was anything the organization could do to help. So I told him about the Trichotillomania Learning Center, and he went ahead and wrote a check right then and there. I was floored! The support was incredible. I realized I hadn't given people enough credit. Everyone has something they're dealing with and when they meet someone who is vulnerable about their own issues, most people can respect that and want to be supportive. It took a huge weight off my shoulders and suddenly I realized I could talk to people about my trichotillomania. I may not tell everyone I meet, but if it comes up in conversation, I'm not going to lie or hide it.

My only regret about telling the local paper my story was that the writer turned it into a story about me being a "victim" and looking for a support group. In reality, I was trying to show that I wasn't a victim, and in fact no one with trich should feel like a victim. They shouldn't be ashamed, and it's ok to ask for help. Lastly, she didn't even mention the Trichotillomania Learning Center in the article. That bothered me more than anything! I wanted people with trich who had never read about it before to know where to go for information.

But in the end, the article allowed several people to reach out to me, and I began my first support group. It was cut short after a few months because my husband and I decided to move to Florida to be closer to family. However, a few months after moving I attended the Trichotillomania Learning Center's annual conference which was being held in my backyard in Orlando, Florida. I met some wonderful women and started another support group, until we moved back to Syracuse a year later.

It was through my interactions with other hair pullers, and opening myself up to my family, friends and co-workers that I realized this disorder does not define me. It truly was a turning point in my life. There is so much more to who I am as a person than my hair pulling. It was around this time that I no longer worried about whether or not people were looking at my eyes. I began to forget that I was missing lashes and brows. I could be myself and pursue my dreams without this issue weighing me down.

Ten years later and I have defined myself in a ton of other ways besides trich:

- Married to a wonderful man and we are continually trying to improve our communication and develop a life plan that reflects our values of love, compassion and social justice
- Reached my dream of earning a master's degree
- Have an amazing career in human resources
- Struggling through fertility issues, my husband and I are pursuing adoption to build our family and are so excited to finally become parents
- We have been blessed financially, can pay our bills on time, and have always had a roof over our head and food on the table

- I write a blog about faith, culture, and my identity in Jesus
- I have overcome my fear of public speaking, including giving my testimony at church about how God has helped me through the struggles in my life, including my trichotillomania and fertility issues.
- I am an advocate... for women particularly who live in a society that defines them by how they look or if they parent. I advocate that all women are valuable whether or not they have hair and whether or not they can conceive and bring a pregnancy to term.
- I've overcome social anxiety and have a wonderful group of close friends after not having many friends at all in childhood.
- My family means everything to me and I'm so blessed to have their support and love in everything I do.

I'll say it again. Trichotillomania *does not* define me as a person. It is a small part of the puzzle that makes up who I am. I do not want to pull my hair forever, but it's something that has made me more compassionate towards other people. I particularly feel an affinity with women and men with self-image issues. I know what it's like to feel ugly. I know what it's like to not feel "normal." I know what it's like to feel like you don't live up to society's standards. I know what it's like to feel out of control.

But through the years I have also learned what it's like to share your story with someone and realize you're not alone. I also know what it's like to have someone fall in love with you and continue to love you when you have hair and when you don't. I know what it's like to go pull free for months, and realize, even after a relapse, that if I've gone pull free once, I can certainly do it again (and I have!).

I recognize that I may never be 100% pull free, but I have the tools I need to pursue a recovery that includes reduced pulling, reduced urges, and the ability to cope with anxiety in new and creative ways that do not involve pulling my hair from my body.

Some days are certainly easier than others. Heck, some months are easier than others! But I honestly believe that something good is supposed to come out of our struggles. I'm sharing my story because I believe in education and advocacy. Millions of people pull their hair yet no one talks about it. People are ignorant to what goes on with those with trich. The more who are aware, the more comfortable people with trich will feel being themselves. But the more it stays hidden and unknown, the more a stigma will be attached.

We with trichotillomania (and other body-focused repetitive behaviors) shouldn't have to feel ashamed for engaging in a coping mechanism to relieve anxiety, stress and boredom. We shouldn't have to feel ashamed for not living up to society's arbitrary rules of beauty. Instead we should be using our stories to help others going through the same or similar struggles. Of course, each person's level of comfort for sharing and educating is different. For some it may just be sharing with their significant other. For some it's their immediate family, and for some like myself, I blog about it and share it with whoever wants to listen. Neither one way is better or worse. But I will say completely hiding trich from the people in your life is not healthy. Anytime people have to hide a part of themselves, it only exacerbates the issue.

So this is who I am: a successful, sometimes anxious, sometimes confident woman, who sometimes pulls my hair. For those who haven't heard of trichotillomania before: it's not a crazy disorder. It's more of an addiction than anything else. Some people overeat. Some people do drugs. Some people exercise. Some people smoke cigarettes. Some people gamble. For those of us with trichotillomania, we pull our hair. It helps us numb out; forget what's going on in our lives. For me specifically, it has helped me refocus when my life feels out of control. When I'm sick, anxious or bored, pulling my hair brings me back to some kind of balance. We all do this in one way or another, engage in a shameful behavior that makes us feel better for the moment, but disappointed once we're done. But the way it manifests looks different for each individual.

When you see someone who colors in their eyebrows, or doesn't have any lashes, or wears a wig, be kind. Look them in the eye with respect and care. All we want is to be treated like everyone else. We don't want to be seen for our hair (or lack thereof), but for our character, our heart, and our love. Isn't that really all that matters when our lives are all said and done?

*I can be found blogging at www.lunamarshall.com.

5
WHAT TTM TAUGHT ME
CINTIA, LATE TWENTIES, ARGETINA

"I'll find a way or I will create." —Anibal Barca

Learning is an engine that supports life. Unfortunate, painful, or difficult experiences can be salvaged and transformed into something positive, something good and productive. In short, this skill of transformative can be learned. I am convinced that TTM has come into my life to teach me.

In order to understand a particular situation, I've learned I have to start at the beginning. I do not remember the exact moment, but I know I was 15 years old when I began pulling my hair. During the first few times, I just removed a dozen hairs watching television. When I studied for a test, the behavior was magnified, and I removed huge swaths of hair from my bangs.

When I try to explain the feelings I had during this behavior, I can say there was no pleasure in the act and no pain either. I would describe it as an accumulation of energy in the body that must be temporarily downloaded.

The period after high school, my pulling was worse. My parents raised me by sometimes criticizing me and sometimes ignoring me, and I became an insecure person. I started several university degrees, until I decided on History. At that time, the hair pulling became an almost ritual act. I got up early to study and while reading, I selected the fingertips that would pluck that first hair of the day. I became a little more aware of what I was doing, and the activity became more enjoyable, but above all, felt inevitable. After each morning, I looked around the chair where I'd been sitting and studying, and my hair covered the floor. I swept up the mess with much anguish and anxiety.

Every obligation that appeared in my life was like a heavy backpack because I was not able to deal with it due to my insecurity. Each hair pulled represented an obligation (an exam, for example) that distressed me, and that is why I removed it from my head.

I began to find good tricks to hide the bald areas, but sometimes even those didn't work. My immediate circle of family and friends noticed it. The only reactions that they gave were to ask me to do nothing or ignore the problem. Having to comb my hair a certain way to hide my bald patches was painful, and I felt was living a lie of my own making. I avoided the problem and did nothing to resolve it.

It took almost ten years for me to hear from a friend of the existence of TTM. She also had it, and I never knew. To find a name for it was a great relief. A year afterward I inexplicably stopped pulling my hair. That time coincided with several situations change in my life. It had been two years since my father died. He was the person who caused me the most anguish and anxiety, as he was the most critical of my actions. I had also already graduated; thereby reducing more of the anxiety I'd felt. I was moving on and starting another stage in life. This, plus the knowledge that my behavior had a medical explanation, helped me get to a point where I could say, "Enough."

Unlike the day I started pulling, I do remember the day I stopped. It was a day like any other—I was watching television and had a freshly plucked hair in my hand. I was almost angry with myself, so I decided to end right there. That would be the last plucked hair that fell to the floor.

I can say that I got it, but my problems were not over. The anxiety that was temporarily dispelled by pulling was now stuck inside me. In a short time I went into a deep depression. And, as is expected in any depressed person, I lost sight of my projects and my hope and faith in myself. I isolated, becoming increasingly suspicious of people, and did not enjoy any activity that involved being around people. I could not practice my profession…my world had fallen apart in every way imaginable.

As an attempt to get help, I decided to start psychological therapy for the first time in my life. I was lucky to find a good professional, who suggested I begin with a radical change. I agreed, not imagining how difficult it would be. All the pain of the first month became, at times, unbearable. I was angry with myself, and I was supposed to let go of the past and mourn. In very little time I was back to pulling my hair.

I must say, this was a very difficult stage, and several times I thought about giving up. However it was worth it to me to not go through this half-heartedly; I focused all the will I could find into making changes. Gradually, I began to notice major shifts. I learned to know myself and to love and accept myself, with or without TTM. I learned to forgive my family reviews, to be a more positive person, and above all, I began to look at life from another point of view. I had renewed interested in fulfilling my dreams and projects; depression was overcome. As for my relapse, it only lasted two months. I stopped pulling and never did it again.

At that time I started looking for information on the disease, I found on the Internet a page that originated in Spain. The coordinator Mr. José Manuel Pérez Quesada had formed a virtual support group. This group supported people from various countries, and the first thing I felt was a great empathy that I had not felt before. In the end, I was not alone; there were more suffering from this condition than I thought. Inevitably I got read some very moving stories, I watched as people desperately asked for help. In a couple of months, the idea of helping others began to haunt me. I had constantly thought about how *I* suffered with this disorder, and how I wished there was someone to lend his ear so that I could vent and not feel so alone. I realized it was useless to keep complaining about and lamenting my condition—instead could do something productive to help others.

Thus in November 2012, I decided to create a blog that I called *"Trichotillomania – Argentina."* Before the first moment of publication, I was so afraid of what might happen, fearing prejudice and ridicule. I did not know if I could cope with such exposure. It was Mr. Quesada who encouraged me by showing me how to encourage myself. I will always be grateful that he joined me in this activity, which then brought me so much satisfaction.

I immediately came across men, women, adults, teenagers, parents of children with TTM—people all throughout Latin America and Spain—who now felt could appreciate the feeling of accompaniment. They wrote me asking for help, treatments, specialists, and support groups. Unfortunately, none of that exists in Spanish-speaking countries.

Maintaining the blog is a totally selfless work, but I do it with seriousness and commitment as I have dedicated myself to the dissemination of information and peer support. Currently, the community that has been formed through the blog has over 300 members who constantly receive words of thanks. Personally, this work has given me great satisfaction and has enriched my life. I am finally empowered after those 11 years of silence, of pain, and so many unanswered questions. I found a road full of hope.

I think this journey that I have shared about my experiences has clarified the idea that TTM is a great vehicle for learning for me. Being able to publicly speak about what I experienced is liberating for me, and I know that it can help others. That is a comforting thought.

I think that each of us who suffer from TTM constantly ask why. "Why do I pull my hair?" "Why did not I stop?" "Why me?" I'm sure that the answer is different for each of us and cannot be found anywhere other than our interior. I also know that the answer is not an end in and of itself, because the answer to why you have or do not have TTM is not what is most important. The question is just the way to build a new road. In my case, the *why* became an engine which put me in motion, preventing conformity with my fears and what I had been told to do.

Today I can say that in any area of my life, when a difficulty or an obstacle presents itself and I am not capable of achieving my goals, I turn on my engine of *why*. I ask myself, if I could cope with all the years I suffered, felt alone, misunderstood, neglected; if I could restore faith in my lost dreams and myself; then, why will I not overcome this, too? There is always a means to achieve what you want. Things can often be difficult, but anything is possible.

*I can be found blogging at www.tricotilomania-argentina.blogspot.com.ar

6
SO MUCH MORE
JARRAH, LATE TWENTIES, CANADA

I went through a lot of changes when I was about nine years old – some good and some not so good. My family was preparing to move from a suburb of Vancouver, Canada to a tiny island with only 700 people. I got my period for the first time. My dog had a litter of seven adorable puppies. I finished Brownies and started Girl Guides (similar to Girl Scouts). And, totally unconnected, I developed trichotillomania: the hair pulling disorder that will probably end up being part of me for the rest of my life.

Now I'm 27, a gainfully-employed communications professional, a cat-loving uber-nerd, an occasional TV commentator, a feminist activist and award-winning blogger.

I wanted to share my story because I know what it was like to go through feeling alone, freakish and all-around horrible about my hair-pulling. I hope that by talking about my experience I can show that trich doesn't have to be a barrier to fulfillment.

It took me quite a while to learn that lesson for myself. Back when I was nine, I didn't have much information to go on when I started pulling out my eyelashes, for no obvious reason. My mom was quite alarmed and took me to the doctor, who guessed my eyes were probably itchy and gave me this tiny tube of goopy cream to put on my eyelids. Of course, that was not the issue.

Not long after that, I started pulling my eyebrows as well. It seems to be very hard for someone without trich to understand but it felt really good. In the spots where I pulled, new stubby hairs would come in and those felt even better to pull. Pulling and fiddling with the hairs I had just pulled kept me feeling calm and in control.

In Grade 5 I was sitting around a table at school, eating lunch with some classmates when a friend of mine, Ashley, pointed across the table at another girl and said, "You have an eyelash on your cheek. You get to make a wish."

The other girl looked happy to hear this. She immediately took the eyelash off of one cheek, shut her eyes, and blew it off the tip of her finger. I had never seen this before, but it made a big impression. For at least a year, every time I pulled I placed the eyelash on the tip of my finger, closed my eyes, and blew it away.

I wished for more friends. I wished for the boys at school to stop teasing me. I wished to do well on assignments. I wished to not have to clean my room. I am slightly embarrassed to admit I wished very hard at one point to meet the Backstreet Boys. I even, occasionally, wished to stop pulling out my eyelashes.

Around the time I was 10 years old the other kids started noticing the gaps in my eyebrows. I remember a trio of dark-haired girls in Girl Guides, as we sat cross-legged on the floor of the school gymnasium, whispering at me that I was a freak and pointing to my eyebrows. I was a really shy kid and already being bullied at school for my clothes and other things, and this just made it worse. I felt exposed and deeply ashamed.

My mom's worry about how this was hurting my looks didn't help. I know she meant well when she pointed out how beautiful my eyelashes had been; even now that I had a trichotillomania diagnosis from another doctor, my mom didn't understand why I couldn't stop. But it certainly wasn't because I wasn't aware of the consequences. I knew how bare and puffy my eyes looked and I felt a deep sense of pain, guilt and failure. I didn't know how to stop and each day I was reminded that everyone saw how ugly I thought I was making myself.

Research shows most people with trichotillomania are girls and women like me. It's tough for everyone, but girls grow up with constant messages in pop culture and advertising telling them they have to look a certain way. Speaking from experience, it feels terrible to be a girl with already low self-esteem looking at mascara ads and realizing you have no eyelashes to even put mascara on.

When something like trichotillomania leaves girls or women with bald patches on their head or gaps in their eyelashes, many withdraw. If someone with trich doesn't feel their elaborate beauty routine is enough to let them fit in, they may isolate themselves from work, school and/or medical care.

At that point in my life from about age 10 to 13, I was mostly able to cover up the hair loss enough by penciling in my eyebrows and wearing eyeliner. But some kids have eagle eyes for anything unusual about you and my hair loss continued to be a target for bullying. One boy in my French class sat behind me and whispered in my ear nearly every day, "*Freak, ugly, whore, freak, ugly, freak…*"

When my parents separated when I was 13 I went into counseling. In addition to issues around the divorce, my counsellor and I tried to tackle the trich. We tried having me wear gloves at times to make it harder to pull. We tried a reward system with prizes if I could go pull-free and a style of aversion therapy where I snapped an elastic band on my wrist when I wanted to pull. We analysed my patterns and tried to develop new mantras. I also tried hypnotherapy. Nothing worked for very long and I still felt like a monstrous creation.

I threw myself into school, because I was good at it and also because my teachers were the only people in my life who didn't seem to notice or care about my hair-pulling. My parents did the absolute best they could with the knowledge they had. They loved me and supported me but my mom's worrying about me reinforced the idea I already had that something was wrong with me. My teachers were the only people I felt valued me and trusted me to succeed.

Partly through the encouragement of a Social Studies teacher in grade 11, I got involved in politics. After studying various party platforms, I joined the New Democratic Party, which had just been voted out of our provincial government and replaced by a much more conservative party. The people I met in the local party association were another group who didn't care about my hair. What they cared about were my values, my ideas and my ability to pitch in and volunteer.

More importantly, political work got me thinking outside my tiny world. I remember getting to go to a big conference in the provincial capital, Victoria, where I met a bunch of other young people who all cared about the issues I cared about, like the environment and fighting cuts to women's centres and helping families in poverty. They were mostly in university and thought it was cool that a high-schooler cared enough about the world around her to get involved in politics. It blew my mind that anyone could think anything I did was cool. It felt amazing.

In 2003 I graduated high school and got accepted to the University of British Columbia. The more I was in this new, more adult world, the less people noticed or cared about my hair-pulling. I was getting better at penciling in replacement eyebrows, but I think it was more that I had grown up and so had my peers. Finally, I was starting to feel like I had worth as a human being and that, just maybe, it was possible for trich not to change that.

Through high school I'd figured my trich was part of my problem of being unable to get a boyfriend. At that time it was devastating because I believed that having a boyfriend was so important, that it was the ultimate thing that could legitimate me.

In university I dated guys and had my first long-term relationship and while some of them were curious about it and wanted to know if they could help, no one was disgusted or stopped going out with me because of my trich.

Part-way through university I stopped feeling the urge to pull my eyelashes and they all grew back. Even though I'm not sure why it happened, I'm glad my eyes are no longer unprotected.

I tried new things periodically: more hypnotherapy, online support groups, supplements, wearing fake nails, even SSRI medication. The longest I ever went pull-free was two weeks. Whenever I tried to stop I was overwhelmed with anxiety and it required a ton of mental energy to monitor my urges and stop myself from pulling.

The biggest challenge is that I always have access to the tools to keep up the behaviour: my hands and my hair. If you have trich and you want to pull hard enough, it is very easy to give in and do so.

I haven't totally given up on trying to go pull-free again but it's not the highest priority for me at this time. After all, I'm really busy, and I now know that I'm a pretty kick-ass, loveable person regardless of how much hair I have. Becoming a feminist and realizing how much of my shame around trich was tied into toxic messages about how women should look definitely helped.

Unfortunately, although I now have full eyelashes, I started pulling hair from my head a couple of years ago to the point where I have large bald patches on the back of my neck and patchy areas around the crown of my head.

When you see me day to day you might notice my hair looks a little off. Maybe it moves a bit funny or it's just too put-together. Earlier this year I appeared as a regular youth election pundit and the women at the TV studio occasionally remarked that my hair always looks perfect. That's because it's not real; it's a wig.

I made the decision to start wearing a wig last fall because I could no longer find a hairstyle that hid the patchy areas. I was conflicted because I do want to end the stigma associated with illnesses like trichotillomania and hiding it to meet beauty ideals is problematic for a feminist like me. On the other hand, the wig protects most of my hair from pulling. Even more importantly, it lets me set boundaries on when I want to talk about my disorder and who I want to talk about it with.

I'm trying to talk about it on my own terms. Earlier this year I outed my trich on my blog, gender-focus.com. I was so nervous I barely slept the night before it was set to be posted. I was afraid my friends and coworkers would look at me differently. I pictured those three dark-haired Girl Guides pointing and whispering, only they were my colleagues. It felt like I was going to be walking out onto a ledge by doing this.

But it was important for me to talk about it and basically say to the world: "I am a person with trichotillomania and I am not ashamed of who I am." It was also important for me to help educate those who don't quite get it – the parents who are like my mom once was or the well-meaning friends – who ask "why don't you just stop?"

I told them if they want to help, to help let others know they're not alone, to keep trying to learn and understand, and to value us as whole people and trust us to deal with it in our own way and ask if we ever do want support.

The response to me telling my story to my family, friends and coworkers was the exact opposite of my fears. It was so overwhelmingly supportive it moved me to tears. I heard from many friends and acquaintances who had trich but were successfully hiding it in secret like I had been, and it felt great but also a bit sad to know we'd been feeling so needlessly isolated from each other before then. In addition from comments from other trichsters sharing their stories with me in return, here are some of the comments I treasured most:

> From one of my long-time best friends: "You keep amazing me in new and wonderful ways. Thanks for having the courage and maturity to share – love you even more for it!"

> From my boss: "Thanks Jarrah. Your courage is an example for the rest of us."

> From one of my sisters: "Thanks for explaining this in a clear and open manner. I didn't know much about this before, or what you were going through. What struck me most is when you said you reached a point where you could see yourself to be a kick-ass loveable person. Truth is, those who are close to you have known this all along. And I'm super happy that you reached this place and will continue to grow and shine and kick some ass."

I also agreed to go back to the morning TV show where I'd

finished my pundit gig and talk about trich. Because that's the path I'm on now: there is so much more to me than trich, but I'm not ashamed about my disorder and I don't want to lie to people. I want to be open about who I am and try to help end the stigma and shame associated with trich.

*I can be found blogging at www.gender-focus.com
Or find me on Twitter: @jarrahpenguin

7
ALWAYS WORTH IT
SEBASTIAN, THIRTIES, CANADA

"What comes, let it come. What stays, let it stay. What goes, let it go" - Papaji

Imagine you woke up one day, and without explanation, you began pulling out your hair. What would you think was wrong with you? Imagine that despite your best efforts, you continued to pull, and pull, and pull—hour after hour, day after day. How demented and defective might you feel? Imagine how lonely and isolating it would be, as you, filled with shame, tried everything in your power to hide and divert all attention from your condition. What would people think of you if they ever found out you pulled? This isn't like feeling depressed or anxious. You pull out your hair, you've bitten and eaten your hair, and you do it on purpose. There is nothing, nothing you can do to stop it. You are insane.

I have trichotillomania. I have been pulling my hair for the last 10 years, and I am beginning to believe that it is something that may always pass in and out of my life for a long time to come. I have three spots (not of my choosing, trust me) that I tend to pull from: my crown, and behind each ear. For the last few years nearly all of my pulling has been localized to my crown, which has ranged from being completely bald to considerably thinner than any of the surrounding hair. And even during the weeks or months where I manage to abstain or manage the pulling that I do, my crown struggles to heal from the countless hours spent obsessing, pulling, and ripping at that spot.

I began pulling my hair when I was in my first year of undergraduate university, which I've heard is quite late to develop a condition that commonly begins sometime during adolescence. Countless times I have thought about what set off this condition and whether or not there was a "critical moment" when this all came to pass. I have yet to find such an event, and over the years I've convinced myself that looking back and trying to find one would be a pretty useless endeavour; I'm not a "root cause" (pardon the pun) kind of guy. What I do know is that my hair pulling coincided with an incredibly stressful period in my life: living alone for the first time, changing course direction in university, tension and difficulties in my family and significant relationships. And I think the tie that binds all these seemingly inevitable experiences together was my inability or reluctance (haven't decided) to manage the storm I was feeling. I bottled it up, didn't communicate my vulnerability to very many people; I never dealt with it. This is not to say that all hair pulling is the result of some extreme emotional upheaval, or imply that it may have been preventable, but given that pulling does have a significant emotional component for me, I am not surprised such a thing would surface during this period of my life. It really was a point ripe for the breakdown of any of my old coping strategies and the emergence of a silent suffering that manifested the struggle I had through it all.

It was years from the time I started pulling to the time that I found out this condition even had a name. Even though I had spent years studying psychology, trichotillomania never came up in any of my coursework. I have always wondered what kept me from reaching out or searching to see if the condition I'd had for years was experienced by anyone else. As perplexing as it may sound, I think a part of me never acknowledged that I had trich; or maybe I had the belief that it was a fleeting oddity, something similar to a cold that I picked up somewhere and would eventually go away. A part of me also knows that I was too ashamed to admit that something like this could ever happen to me, and I became convinced that I must be alone to suffer with it. Whatever it was, I was ready to accept it for years. Ignorance was bliss. Or, so I thought.

My absolute worst moment with trich was the first time my pulling no longer left any hope that the damage could be covered up or hidden—the day that all my thinning hair finally became an unmistakable, unchangeable bald patch. That day I pulled out that last clump of hair, looked in the mirror and saw what I had done, I felt the sting of fear, shame, and grief overwhelm me. *Look what you've fucking done now*, I said to myself. No amount of combing, hairstyling, or hair product could cover up what I had done. It flooded me, the throat-clenching realization of having to go out into the world marked with this condition. That was my worst moment with trich.

I've had lots of other bad moments with trich too. I'm "fortunate" that as a guy, and because of the location of my hair pulling sites, I've always been able to defer any suspicion or questioning by falling back on male-pattern baldness. I typically say something like: "You've seen my dad right? Went grey by 25 and nearly bald by 30. I guess I must have his genes." That works well enough to stall any continued questioning, but to this day it brings the condition that I have tried so hard to distance myself from to the very forefront of my awareness. You would not know it on the outside, but inside I am turning into an emotional wreck, as the years of effort, self-acceptance, and struggle fall apart. I shatter instantly.

I have always felt an incredible sense of shame having trichotillomania. To this day, I still struggle with the reason this condition found its way to me. There are days when I beg for it to go away and times I wish that something a little less "insane" could have developed instead. Wouldn't it be easier if I just had high anxiety? There must be something else that's a little bit more fashionable than a condition that causes me to spend hours upon hours tearing, ripping, and pulling at my own hair, right?

Part of the shame that I continue to experience is how futile I have been in "curing" trich. I am smart, I have had a lot of successes and overcome a lot of challenges, but not being able to "fix" the fact that I pull out my hair has always plagued my mind and made me feel so awfully incompetent. Trich reminds me on a daily basis of its presence; it seems to insult the fact that despite all the mastery I have over so many other areas of my life, I am still so weak and powerless over it.

To be completely transparent, I am ashamed that even as I write this piece, even after all my research and readings, my thesis completed on trichotillomania, the conferences I've attended, and all my personal work as a therapist; I am still pulling. There are still nights where I become incredibly ashamed of the condition that I have, where I become stressed or anxious enough that I return to pulling, and days where I am still brought to pieces by this condition.

This is my story with trich. I have done a lot of reflecting about how sharing my struggles and story could be very discouraging to others. After all, there are days where I still pull, so my success can't be defined by abstinence. I don't know how accepting I am of the condition all the time, so my success there waxes and wanes on a daily basis. And I even struggle with feeling beautiful in any appreciable way because of trich. I hope my last section helps create a shift in those who still struggle intensely with trich from struggle to success.

I believe my success comes from taking trich along in my journey through life. In a very abstract way, this condition has become a guide that helps shape me and challenges me to do things I otherwise may never have done. It teaches me how to pay more attention to my body and my emotional state. It teaches me to be more aware of the times when I am uncomfortable, dwelling in thought, or living too much in my worries and fears. Trich, the most vulnerable part of me, strengthens my mind and actions to strive towards higher awareness and beneficial acts. It demands I show greater patience, gentleness, and compassion towards myself. When I am living too unconsciously and unkindly, trich meets me with its presence and challenges me towards right action.

This is my journey with trich. My hope in writing this to you is to share that trich is still an incredible challenge in my life, and I hope that for some of you reading this, that something in my continued struggle resonates with your own difficulties having this condition. I could not honestly write this if I had lined my story with embellished enthusiasm or hope that this condition will leave me. Rather, in living with the idea that trich may never fully leave, I tried to look at how this condition has given me the ability be more attuned to myself and give me greater insight into my actions, emotions, and thoughts. And if I can offer one thing to take away from all of this, it is that trich is a challenge, and that may not be a bad thing. It might in fact be a very affirming thing. Challenges shape and define the people assigned to face them. They help mold us to the people we want to be, and they test our limits and can give us incredible insight about who we are. We can learn more from one hair pulled than we can from a lifetime of perfection. Trich can be an instrument to help guide our lives in the best possible direction. And to strive and suffer for self-awareness is always worth it.

8
LOUD SILENCE
KENSINGTON ROSE, THIRTIES, TEXAS

I'm not exactly sure how old I was when I started pulling, but I must have been pretty young because I know it was a well established habit by first grade. I became aware I was doing something different than other children in first grade. This was back before kindergarten was mandatory and I had stayed home up until then.

It didn't take long for me to catch on that I was different. I remember overhearing my mom say something to the teacher about my "bad allergies" causing the "problem." Apparently the teacher asked my mom why I didn't have eyelashes. I don't think that my mom and I talked about it too much and until then, I certainly wasn't aware I had bad allergies and a problem.

However, you're never too young for that sinking feeling in the pit of your stomach. It's the one that stays the same at any age, the one that silently screams something is really, really wrong, and life will never be the same. I had that feeling that day in first grade. In fact, I'm not sure it ever entirely goes away.

When school pictures arrived we all got our packets and began to pass around the pictures. Within a few moments, the close-up picture of my face glared back at me. The pale skin on my eyelids was interspersed by patches of long beautiful, black eyelashes. The other kids weren't like that. Instantly, I realized that my eyes were different from others and that was the problem. Other kids didn't pull out there eyelashes. This newfound awareness resulted in an immediate promise to myself to stop pulling and let them grow back. Little did I know that day in first grade began a lifelong battle I would fight with myself.

Battle time came sporadically throughout the day in various places, but at night, my bedroom was ground zero. My room had Care Bear wallpaper and colorful bunk beds that I was really proud of. I let my teddy bears and dolls sleep on the top bunk, since it was by far the choice location, and I slept underneath. On my nightstand was a stack of Berenstain Bear books and a Cabbage Patch lamp. The lamp and I spent many long nights together as I painstakingly tried to resist the urge to pull another eyelash. The dim glow of the light seemed to highlight each little failure all throughout the night. Each night was the same routine: I took a bath, brushed my teeth, and had a bedtime story. Then I'd try to go to sleep, but instead spent hours attempting to resist the urge to pull. I inevitably lost my nightly battle and woke up to feel the naked skin of an eyelid free of eyelashes. And to my absolute horror, the harder I tried to stop, the more I wanted to do it.

I wanted to pull at school, on the playground, and any time I could free a hand to inch its way to my eyes. I would pull while reading, watching TV, or trying to fall asleep. Sometimes it was a very focused activity with each lash carefully examined. The root fascinated me. I ran it along my lips and ate it. On other occasions, I just zoned out, time and surroundings ceasing to exist.

In childhood, the pulling continued despite my best efforts to get control of it. This bizarre behavior was something I couldn't begin to understand or explain. My mom seem to think I would eventually "just grow out of it," much like some kids eventually outgrow their pacifier or thumb-sucking, but this was totally different. Not only did I *not* outgrow it, but it also got worse. The small patches of missing eyelashes grew wider, and by fourth grade I was upset enough by my appearance to ask my mom how to cover up those bare spots on my eyes. That began my daily regimen of applying eyeliner, glue and fake eyelashes. I still adhere to that regimen to this day.

Now, I'm 35, married, have a master's degree, full time job and three dogs I affectionately call my "'fur" babies. The hardest part for me is that trich is like a war I battle and lose every night. I own my own house, pool, car, and other material items, but this disease owns my eyes' lashes and brows.

I am as bewildered as anyone else as to why I can't seem to "get a grip" on the behavior. All I can say is that it doesn't feel like a choice. It doesn't hurt. In fact it feels really good - the closest thing I can compare it to is similar to when you feel the tickle right before you sneeze, and you just want to hurry up and sneeze to make that feeling go away. Then it's actually a total relief to just sneeze and relieve the itch. That's part of what makes "just stopping" so difficult. Could you promise yourself never to sneeze again? Can you will yourself to never itch again? Another thing I would compare it to is the uncontrollable cough that occurs when as when you swallow something the "wrong way." Would you look at someone who was choking and tell them they have a choice not to choke? Would you ask them why they just couldn't stop choking? Would you make them promise to never choke again?

Yes, I realize at this point those who don't deal with trich might be thinking, *well choking is totally different.* And what I'm trying to explain is that what might be right for others' bodies, is not right for mine. It may sound silly, and I know if I didn't have this condition I would probably just roll my eyes if someone said they couldn't stop pulling. But, the sensation of pulling my eyelashes is equivalent to sneezing or choking for me.

I have often wondered if this itchy sensation is an indication that this is some sort of allergic, dermatological, or other biological condition, however the medical community seems pretty insistent that it is strictly a mental illness. I agree as it does seem to have similarities with other conditions such as Obsessive Compulsive Disorder, and I definitely feel a reduction in anxiety from pulling. From what I've read, most people that have trich seem to suffer or at least have had bouts of depression. But which came first, the depression or the trich? Does depression trigger the trich or does having trich (and therefore keeping secrets, feeling ostracized, ugly, and like a failure) lead to depression? I started pulling so young I have no idea if I was depressed by preschool, but I think I probably was a very shy and sensitive child and easily became anxious.

I certainly don't dispute times of stress exacerbate the condition, but then stress can make almost any condition worse. From a physical perspective, I've always wondered why the pulling does not hurt me. It really doesn't hurt. It's as though my nerves lack a pain sensation, or at least, they are different in that area. I wouldn't compare my experience to people who cut themselves to feel the pain and get endorphins because I experience no pain. I'm sure about this because I've tried pulling in other places on my body to see if I could find a less obvious substitute for my face. But reproducing the sensation in other places didn't work. Trying to pull from another part of my body results in a resounding *ouch!* just like other folks. That helped me understand how it must seem to most people. I can see why someone might compare pulling to cutting or hurting yourself, but all I can tell you is that for me, I think there is a hole in that theory. It just doesn't hurt. Trust me, nobody more than I wished it did, because then it would be much easier to stop.

From what I have been able to research there seems to be a mixed bag of trichotillomania sufferers. Some report that their condition started during times of abuse, or they can trace when they began to pull after a single traumatic experience. Others have experienced a generally "bad childhood" or rough patch in life, and then others swear that they started during otherwise very happy, low stress times. Perhaps there are both biological and psychological aspects to the condition.

I do think, at least in part, trich is likely a coping mechanism for my uncomfortable feelings. I should probably also tell you a little bit about my home life. My parents were married until I was in junior high, so my early years were spent in a modest home in a small suburb of Dallas. It was not a happy home though. They both readily admit that my dad had really never wanted to have kids, while my mother would have loved a large family. They had my sister seven and half years before me, and apparently, from what I've heard from others as an adult, from a young age she was very hesitant to be independent. My mother, knowing that she wouldn't have very many children since my father wasn't interested, doted on my sister, fulfilling her every need and desire. This dynamic created a strong lifelong relationship of dependence that still exists to this day.

The surprise of my conception years later was probably met with, at best, a reluctant welcome. My father openly admitted he would have preferred my mother have an abortion, but she refused even though by the time I came along my sister was a master of occupying all my mom's time and energy. I was a difficult baby with clubfeet and colic. My feet required weekly visits to the doctor to have huge casts applied, and I was never a good sleeper. (I'm still an insomniac.) I think my mother's vision of being a stay at home mom involved enjoying beautiful times with a multitude of sweet little children at her feet. Her illusions were shattered, first by my sister; a difficult and strong willed child that she was ill prepared to handle with little support; then further by me, a needy and demanding infant, complete with weekly doctor appointments and crying fits from the foot pain and colic. I was not the picture perfect Gerber baby she had envisioned.

As she accepted the doctor's appointments and health issues she began to see that she could make having sickly dependent children a lifestyle. She insisted on being a stay at home mom because after all, her children were always sick or needing a doctor's visit. My dad had pretty much decided that if he were going to support a stay at home wife then he would rarely come home. He kept busy by working three jobs and playing racquetball with his friends. Most of my childhood he left before I woke up and came home after I was already tucked into bed (where I was usually not sleeping but dealing with my own struggles). While I knew he loved me, he was from the generation that believed as long as they provided for their family their job was done, and that was all he was interested in doing.

By nature, Dad can be the life of the party, but he can also be an outspoken and critical person. I wouldn't have dared confided in him about my strange behavior. From fourth grade on he was just one more person I had to hide the effects of my bizarre behavior from. We have a friendly relationship now and see each other weekly for lunch, but I still wouldn't want him to ever see me without my makeup. Putting on my mask is an essential daily task. I know he knows of it, but we rarely speak about it. He can't seem to wrap his brain around why an otherwise strong, intelligent daughter of his can't stop pulling, and I can't explain it for him. I think he feels like the money spent on counseling in my youth was "wasted" since I'm not "fixed." Now he doesn't know what else to say.

Throughout my childhood (and life) I went through phases where the pulling would lessen, but I don't think I've ever totally stopped. The closest I ever came to stopping was a period of nearly two years in fourth and fifth grade when I came down with a mysterious ailment. My arms and legs ached constantly. I went from being involved in competitive dance and gymnastics, and even jumping on our trampoline daily, to not wanting to move from the couch. My arms would often ache so badly that I needed help brushing my teeth or hair. Pulling virtually ceased because I was always either asleep or simply needing help managing the basics of life. I was dragged from doctor to doctor and given hundreds of test but nothing was ever found. Within months, I was extremely thin and weak and could no longer walk to the mailbox.

One doctor we saw suggested I start swimming to gain strength, so on Saturdays I began going along with Dad to the gym where he played racquetball. They had an indoor pool where I began swimming short distances very slowly but eventually building up to one mile. My dad would often take me to breakfast after the gym, and I really looked forward to our weekly swimming and waffles date. It wasn't long before I was clearly healthy enough to return to school. Unfortunately, during the time I had been sick, they had re-zoned our neighborhood, and so instead of rejoining the kids I went to elementary school with I had to go to a different elementary school for sixth grade and then a different junior high. Once again, the pulling restarted, and I had a whole new group of friends to make. Which also meant I had a whole new set of people I needed to ensure never discovered my secret.

Junior high was a very rough time for me and unfortunately I added another secret to the mix: bulimia. After I was so thin, when I got well my weight spiked rapidly. Even though I was probably a normal weight, I got right back into dance and it didn't take long before I felt huge.

My anxiety ran high all day. There was barely enough time between classes to go to your locker or the bathroom before the tardy bell rang, much less find a private place to re-glue my eyelashes or re-apply makeup after gym. Keeping up appearances was a huge added stress to my adolescence, and looking back I never had a friend or family member I felt I could really talk to. My mother and my sister knew about the pulling, but if I tried to talk to them about it, they would flit between acceptance and teasing. I had friends at school, but junior high girls are notoriously fickle. I was always worried that if even just one of them found out my secret, I would be left with no one to sit at with lunch and become the notorious butt of endless jokes. I worked very hard to protect everyone else I knew or came into contact with from having to see my awful reality.

If I slept over a friend's house, I made sure I was the last one to fall asleep and the first to wake up so I could fix my face. I went swimming, but I was careful to avoid things that got my face wet, and I always had my emergency fix-it kit that included eyelashes, glue, eyeliner, and later, an eyebrow pencil, too. I still never leave home without my make-up and keep back-up kits in my car and desk at work. In middle school my general daily routine was: glue on my eyelashes in the morning, went to school where I played the role of good girl who kept to herself except for necessary socialization and then came home to alternate between phases of socializing after school or bulimia, and then went to bed where I usually would read and pull until I finally drifted off to sleep.

As an adult, I have gone to counseling a few times, and I am an avid reader. If pressed, I think I would now say that being "fixed" could mean different things for different people. For an alcoholic, clearly quitting drinking may be the fix. For a condition such as this (or so many others) where you can't get away from yourself, maybe being "fixed" is learning to accept yourself, to continue to get up day after day, put your makeup on, come home and wash it all off, while listening to that tiny whisper inside you that says you will and *can* do it again tomorrow.

There is so much shame revolving around this disease that I think is hard for people to relate to. If you lose all your hair or a breast from cancer there is little shame in having the cancer itself (though I'm sure embarrassment, fear, and insecurity are present, but that is different than shame). You're simply the victim of a vicious disease and people see you as someone to rally around and support. Not so with trich. You're seen as part of the problem because you're "choosing" the behavior and are not participating in the solution. What could be the support of a friend or family member is often replaced with disgust and impatience. So the shame sinks deeper and the secrecy gets ever more perfected. I feel like I have "Damaged Goods" stamped on my face, and I must cover it up everyday before I leave the house.

Home was also a land of keeping up a facade. My parents' marriage was clearly falling apart and the silence and tension in the house could be cut with a knife. I was left to figure out homework and other activities on my own while mother remained preoccupied with my sister (this isn't just me saying that, I've had numerous people comment on the contrast in my mother's attention towards my sister and I) and my father worked hard to be absent. By the time I was in college I realized my father was more than likely avoiding home to avoid dealing with my mother and sister's drama, but back then, as young children often do, I quickly internalized that there was something so awful about me my own father rarely wanted to be at home. I had all the proof I needed looking back at me in the mirror.

I often found myself pulling while doing homework. Alone in my room and sitting at my desk, homework time became a battle between pulling and attempts at concentration.

We rarely had family meals and I pretty much lived on a steady diet of candy, McDonalds and Chinese food, just making my own schedule and doing my own thing. We rarely had what I now call staples—sandwich ingredients, fresh vegetables or fruit because my mother and sister didn't eat those things, and my dad ate most of his meals outside the home. But we always had a well-stocked pantry of their favorites: mac & cheese, hot dogs, pizza, chips, cookies and cakes. As an adult, I have noticed that when I eat healthy and take care of myself the pulling seems to slow down and I do wonder if my poor eating habits as an adolescent intensified the pulling.

The summer before ninth grade my parents divorced and my mom decided we'd move to Austin. She thought Austin was a cooler city than Dallas—both literally and figuratively. I didn't want to move and asked to stay with my father, who moved closer to his job in Dallas, but he was traveling for work most weeks Monday-Thursday, and he thought I would be better off with my mother.

When they divorced, my sister had lived in her room for two solid years. She literally never came out or left the house since graduating high school. She had a waterbed, bathroom, and a TV easily accessible, and my mother brought her anything she wanted for meals. I didn't catch on at the time, but my mother loved it when we stayed home from school due to sickness. The more ailments my sister could complain about, the more school she missed. Then she was handsomely rewarded with weekend shopping sprees at the mall. My sister was very smart; she made better grades than I did without studying, but my mother insisted she had learning disabilities and other various health issues, which were the reason why she couldn't work, go to college, etc. Looking back, I didn't catch on to the reward system so quickly, because other than math, I liked going to school. It was fun to socialize, play, and learn new things. But eventually I realized that staying home from school due to sickness always equaled a new toy from Toys "R" Us. As a kid, you just accept so many things; I just thought all kids got a new toy if they were sick at home. My sister had no desire to be independent (unlike me), and my father didn't like this arrangement, but seemed to prefer letting my mother and sister do their own thing rather than engage in a conflict.

During the divorce, my mother moved my sister to an apartment near our old home and insisted my father subsidize her, which he begrudgingly did. I have no idea why mom chose to uproot us and move to Austin other than I remember her saying she heard it was a cool town. She chose to rent a duplex on the outskirts of town, in a very undeveloped area where we knew no one. I had two friends in my old the neighborhood that it broke my heart to leave. Our old house had a huge backyard and we had four dogs, which I loved, but my mom gave all of them away, with the exception of one—my beloved Sugar, when she decided to move us. We took very little with us. I brought some clothes, books and my makeup. Once we got there my mother spent her days buying furniture, shopping, exercising and going to church (which we had never done before but apparently she found one with quite the singles group), where she quickly began dating. It was really odd to see my mom dating, especially at a time where I was also becoming interested in dating, and for a while it made me totally uninterested.

Surprisingly, the first year we spent in Austin my eating issues and pulling nearly disappeared. I think I was just excited about a new town, new school, and new beginnings. It was good to be away from my sister who was often mean to me (for example chasing me around the house with a butcher knife or holding me down and putting a water hose in my mouth and plugging my nose and turning it on. I sometimes joke I was waterboarded in my childhood. And my sister stole my stuff). There wasn't much food in the house and I didn't have a car so there was no way I could binge and purge. I could spend my days walking the dog, jogging in the park, and reading. It was lonely, but it was acceptable in my mind to be lonely for the summer since I was in a new town.

As soon as school started, I made a couple of good friends, and I set a goal for myself to make the high school drill team, which I did the following year. While it helped me make friends and stay busy, the focus on my appearance sent my self-destructive habits into a tailspin. The uniforms we wore were revealing, and I felt enormous (at around 85 pounds). Soon, I was purging daily and pulling quickly branched out from my eyelashes to eyebrows. I had only battled eyelash pulling until high school, when the eyebrows became part of the mix. Night after night alone in our duplex was when sleep rarely came and the pulling urges would overcome me. One of those awful nights I pulled until every eyelash was gone and somehow my hand moved up to my eyebrows and wouldn't stop. The next day I skipped school to go to the drugstore and look into eyebrow makeup. From that day forward an eyebrow pencil became a permanent staple to my purse. The urge to pull both my lashes and my brows has never ceased.

I was appalled by my own behavior, but had no one in which to confide. I was too afraid to reveal my true self to my new friends at school. I desperately wanted to be liked, letter in dance team, and have a boyfriend. I think I felt that if anyone discovered my secrets none of that would come true. So I became better at hiding my destructive habits and painting on my happy face. It worked for a while, but then my mom met a man at church that invited her to move in, and she announced she would be moving out. I was 16 when I basically started living on my own.

My mom dropped off the rent and some extra money for food, and she nagged my father until he bought me an old car so I could get to school, dance team practice, and my job at a fast food restaurant. (We didn't live close to anything so the only way to get her off the hook for carting me around was to give me transportation.) Meanwhile my sister continued to live and be supported by my parents. She was too scared to drive at 23, so they also gave her money to pay people for rides. I was given the keys to an old Toyota Corolla and told if I wanted to get anywhere I had better figure out how to drive. I was terrified, but in an effort to get to school and acquire food I forced myself to get behind the wheel. My mother moved in with her new boyfriend, only coming by once a week to pay the rent, do laundry (her new boyfriend didn't have a washing machine) and drop off money for me to buy food.

I went for weeks without seeing or talking to her as she typically came by while I was at school. I rarely talked with or heard from my father, and in those days without cell phones or the Internet, any friendships I had back in the town where I grew up were neglected. I suddenly missed my sister and desperately tried to forge a relationship with her, even given how she usually treated me. I also tried reaching out to my father numerous times, but he would always tell me I was better off with my mother. When I told him I was having some problems and missed him he would send money so I could go get counseling, but I doubt he even asked what those problems were. I think he assumed it was petty high school girl stuff, and I could confide in my mother.

Dad says he never dreamed she would leave me alone as much as she did and assumed my complaints were within the realm of normal mother-teenage daughter teenage scenarios. In fact, he had reasoned, maybe we were closer since my sister was further away. But in fact, when my sister no longer needing daily caretaking, my mother decided she was done being a mother. She really made no bones about it, just one day announced she was done and would scold me for being selfish if I asked her to do something she considered unreasonable. To her, it was unreasonable to attend a football game with the other mothers to see me dance or join me for dinner. Never in two years of drill team did she come to one game. My father actually drove down to see me in one of my last games, but unfortunately, it was canceled due to rain.

My poor eating habits and lack of sleep had also started to catch up with me. I had trouble learning and remembering dances, and my memory would go blank during tests. Suddenly I was angry and tired all the time and I didn't know why. The things I had liked—dancing, school, and slumber parties—started to just make me irritable and all seemed stupid.

High school was both a heaven and a hell. Home was lonely and school brought me much needed company and socialization, but I knew no one well enough to be real with them and was extremely conscientious of my weight and appearance. I played the role of the happy high school girl all day and then stayed up until the wee hours of the morning binging/purging and pulling.

I desperately tried to find something else that would comfort me. I tried drinking, smoking, coke, and sex, but none of it brought the relief (albeit temporary) of throwing up and pulling. I realized at 16 that we don't pick our addictions, our addictions pick us. I found my own addictions, purging and picking, so grotesque. In my eyes, I judged myself to be no better than a crack whore, and I believed I was totally powerless against my problems. Looking back I am amazed I was able to do as much as I did despite the way I treated my body and my total lack of guidance from anyone. But at the time I felt totally worthless.

Instead of feeling any pride in all that I was doing—I made honor roll, lettered in drill team, and worked after school—I felt like a total failure because I couldn't quit pulling. Oddly, at the time I didn't at all feel my mother's absence, as her voice was always in my head. "Get it together," or "stop being so selfish," were her favorite phrases during my teen years, and I felt there was something totally inferior about me. Throughout high school, I did not feel worthy of a mother's love or time so it made sense to me that I didn't get it, and I believed it was my own fault.

Many teenagers would have probably loved all the freedom I possessed, and while at times I did, I also found it necessary to give myself strict rules. For example, if I got an 88 on a test I had to purge 12 times that day to "earn" my 100. I also briefly started cutting for a while (that DOES hurt and make for awkward situations on dates), but I never got the same relaxed sensation that I could with pulling and purging, so I stopped.

By eleventh grade I wanted to be finished with high school. After basically living on my own, it seemed ridiculous to have to ask permission to go to the bathroom. One day I just decided I wasn't going to do it anymore. I was looking forward to none of the usual senior year activities. Every day was already so tiring, and they just sounded exhausting, expensive, and a huge reminder of my worthlessness. There would be no one to take a picture of me as I went to prom or insist on ordering senior pictures, so what was the point of asking for a hall pass for another year?

I knew had more than enough credits to get a diploma so I stopped by the office and told them I wouldn't be back, asking them to mail me my diploma. I felt like college could be the place I could get the fresh start I had hoped I would get in high school. I was too young and immature to realize you can't run away from yourself. So, when a glossy brochure from a small women's college arrived in the mail, along with the promise of enough financial aid to make your college dreams come true and an environment full of the camaraderie and support of other women, I immediately applied. I got accepted and bought a one-way ticket to Oakland, California.

These were the days before everyone had a smartphone and without Google in my pocket I had visions of sunny, warm California and weekend trips to the ocean. It's embarrassing to admit now (I Google everything!), but I think I just wanted to get away from my lonely situation so badly I was willing to take a chance. Of course, the old run down college in northern California was nothing like what I expected. With no transportation I was going to have to make friends fast or learn the bus system, which if you know anything about Texans, you know we don't comprehend the concept of public transportation very well.

My little dorm room was single occupancy. I was supposed to have a roommate, but due to some mix up I got an individual room. I had graduated in December so I started mid-semester. I tried to go to the community rooms and be friendly, but after a few tries I found the women uninterested and unaccepting of me. They seemed to think I was a joke. I was the weird girl from Texas that didn't even know which group to try to fit in with. As much as I wanted to be liked I was hesitant to approach all these women. There were groups that were experimenting sexually, or passionate about a cause, or discussing at length the latest demonstration at nearby Berkeley. At the time I wasn't politically savvy or particularly passionate about any certain cause, I just wanted to make some friends and hang out. But instead I found myself surrounded by other girls that seemed just as angry and confused as I was.

My heart hurt as I retreated to my little room. It was like being sentenced to a pulling jail where I could have pizza delivered. My eyelashes could fall off in the community showers, so I didn't risk it. I came and went at odd hours to avoid others. Lonely and disappointed by the college experience, I strengthened my resolve to get an education that would give me the independence I so desired, but that resolve was short-lived.

I had a rude awakening when I realized my financial aid package consisted mostly of loans and not scholarships. The crappy old building I was camping out in turned out to be crazy expensive. I then decided to finish out the semester and return to Texas. I would have to find another, cheaper college, but I still wanted to spend the semester studying and making good grades even if I pulled out every hair on my body. (I didn't, but it was not a happy time). I guess I figured that at least the money I borrowed wouldn't be wasted if my grades were good and the classes would transfer. If presented with the same situation today, I would have cut my losses and left, but I really had nowhere to go and was embarrassed by what I saw as my stupidity. I did make a "friend," if you could call her that. She seemed to need someone to pal around with when her boyfriend was unavailable, and she had a car. She could be mean though. She often told me I looked "Jewish," and by that she meant I needed a nose job. But she drove me places and was a way to get off that dreary campus.

One night our pseudo-friendship blew up at a party she had driven us to. She and her boyfriend had a fight and apparently during it he had mentioned something about me, calling me her "hot friend." She lashed out and attacked me, which took me by complete surprise. I had no idea what I had done, but it was clear it was no longer going to be a fun party, nor did I have a ride back to my dorm. It was late and dark, and I just wanted to get back to my dorm room. With no money and no one to call, I decided to walk back. I walked through some pretty tough parts of Oakland and soon I was followed and attacked. I later learned it was a popular form of rape in the area called a "gang bang." In my intoxicated, emaciated state I was no match to fight back. Fear and shock silenced me. My ridiculous high heels, which I had borrowed from my former friend, did not help me get away.

When I got back to my room I was shocked and nauseated. The dorms were pretty empty because it was a Saturday night. I was so cold and wet from the rain I took a long hot shower and did my best to wash the day and all it's awfulness away. It would be years later in a counseling session for the eating disorder that re-emerged that a therapist would tell me that what happened to me was rape, and it wasn't my fault. At the time I blamed myself.

It was my fault for coming to the school in the first place and not checking things out before I came. It was my fault for wearing a short dress and high heels, for walking alone, and for getting my one friend mad at me even though I had no idea why. I spent the next few days holed up in my little room. I discovered all the money I had, two rolls of quarters of laundry money, was stolen during the attack. I was completely and totally numb, except that pulling, binging, and purging felt good. The rain outside my window felt like the tears I should have been able to cry. There was nowhere I wanted to go or anybody I wanted to see. My former "friend" filled my answering machine with angry Jewish slurs and "stay away from my man" comments (who I could have not had less interest in.) After a few days I had enough; enough showers, enough of my answering machine being filled with angry rants, and enough self-induced solitary confinement.

I emerged from my room and took my answering machine tape to the head of the dorm facilities. Ironically, I reported the missing laundry quarters but said nothing about what had happened otherwise. When I returned to my room, the answering machine's little red light flashed red, and I figured it would be more insults, but I pressed "play" anyway. It was my dad. A business trip was sending him my way and he asked if I'd like him to come visit. With no ally in my corner or even enough quarters to do laundry, I grabbed the phone and called him back. Downplaying my sadness, I told him my grades were good, but I didn't think this was the right place for me. I lied and told him my wallet had just been stolen at a recent trip to McDonald's, leaving me broke. He agreed to send me some money to help, and we made plans for him to come see me. The phone call and the promise of a visit filled me with hope. I anxiously awaited his visit.

We had a great time visiting Alcatraz and Pier 39. We ate and talked the whole day. It was a bit like meeting again for the first time. I think he was surprised by how much I had grown up since early middle school, and he could tell I wasn't happy at the college. He offered to let me come back with him, but I insisted on staying to finish out the semester, not wanting to lose the credits.

I heard back from the head of the dorm services, and she let me know that the student responsible for leaving slurs on my answering machine would be dealt with immediately. I did finish out the semester. About a month later, after I'd returned to Texas, I received a letter from my former friend. It was clearly a forced apology she was told to write by the administration, but I had at least stood up for myself in some small way.

When the semester ended I returned to Austin but knew I wouldn't stay long. I had no interest in returning to my mother's house, nor did her boyfriend now turned husband welcome me. Her new husband made it very clear he didn't like his own children and had no desire to get to know me. My mom had sold the duplex and bought a bigger house in an older, rougher area of town. She moved my sister in, as well as an aunt and a cousin. I tried living there, but my aunt was a relentless pot smoker (I've always hated that smell, it makes me nauseous) and my cousin was struggling with his own sexual identity and holding down a job. My sister had become an adept thief by this point, and if I didn't keep my money and belongings on me or locked in my car they would disappear while I slept. My Corolla was still there, and I called my dad to let him know I wanted to live with him. We agreed I would stay with him for the summer, and I would find another school to attend. I worked the summer at a law office during the day and was a hostess at a restaurant in the evenings. Once I told my father about my aunt and cousin, my he did seemed surprised that my mother had become so distant from me. He agreed I could stay with him whenever I needed too.

I applied and got into another college, and I think my father and I were both surprised by how much we would miss each other once I went off to college. During college my dad and I got to know each other, since I went to his house on school breaks. He still traveled a lot for work, but now that I was a college student, he didn't mind me being at his house alone.

College wasn't easy. Pulling was awful when I studied. I also had several bouts of depression. I worried that no one would ever love or accept me in my damaged state. I saw numerous doctors and tried several different types of medication, but nothing made the pulling any better and a few even made it worse.

Since then, I have taken medication to decrease my anxiety or help me fall asleep when I need to. I did get counseling and overcame my eating disorder, but I still pull. Much of what I included in this story may not seem directly related to the pulling, but I think that a sense of low-self worth, self-hatred, and shame leads to poor choices, and poor choices have their consequences. I don't blame any one particular thing—the trich or the family stuff—but I do hope that others can see how important it is to support one another, even if we don't understand each other.

At 28, after earning a master's degree and starting a new career, I was blessed to meet the man who would be my husband. At 19, he had lost his parents during a violent home invasion, and I was impressed and inspired by his resilience and strength. He seemed to understand that life sometimes deals us awful blows, and the best we can do is persevere and choose to do right despite it all. He loved my light and accepted my darkness. That was a gift I never thought I would receive, nor did I believe I deserved it.

We have now been married for seven years, and I have been in my current career ten. I still pull almost every night and wake up to go through my makeup routine. I don't know if I will ever quit pulling, but I do know that in the grand scheme of things, it's just hair. I still hate that I do it, I still want to change, but I have come to realize that fighting the urges (for me) actually makes them stronger. My best bet is to take care of myself and try to have as little stress in my life as possible, and deal with the stress I do have healthily. I get rest, eat well, exercise and just generally try to live as balanced a life as possible. Once I come home I like to wash my face because my eyes and the area surrounding them feels better clean. Also, if I keep my hands busy until I get tired, it does seem to help me.

When my pulling increases dramatically, I have learned to take that as a sign I need to adjust something in my life. Pulling is like an internal barometer that lets me know when I need to make an adjustment somewhere. It's like a visual scream: *something is wrong here!* I still hope that one day my pulling will greatly decrease, if not cease completely, but I no longer let my pulling urges be the judge and jury of my self-worth and happiness. That alone has been a huge battle for me. Sometimes I have felt like the pulling, some call it the "trich monster," has its own, incredibly powerful voice. I know every person has inner demons and insecurities, but the trich monster is so much more than that. I've heard negative self-talk referred to as the "shitty committee." I've got that, but with trich I have an additional committee member saying: *just pull one more hair, it will be the last one.*

75

It's always a lie.

I still try to hide my missing hair in public, but I have learned I don't have to hide from myself. In my private moments I now try to listen to the loud silence that is the pulling, that is trichotillomania, that is me, that is hair, that is a form of communication.

It is still very hard for me to share my pulling with others, but I handle inquiries better than I used to. I've learned just because someone ask me a question doesn't mean I have to answer. If someone I don't know well asks why don't I have eyelashes or eyebrows I just matter-of-factly say " It's a health issue" or "I prefer to only discuss my health with my family and my doctor" (i.e. none of your business!). I also occasionally have people tell me my eyelashes or eyebrows look "perfect." I used to say something negative in response. Now, I just smile and say thank you. It's a good reminder for me that perfection is always an illusion.

I did have a co-worker ask me one time "Why do you wear fake eyelashes?" and he wasn't doing it to be mean. He was just curious and concerned. I wasn't ready to confide in him so I just paused and said, "Does it matter?" He smiled and responded, "No, it doesn't," and we just sort of chuckled and shrugged and went on our way.

9
ONE BAD HAIR
RACHEL, LATE FORTIES, CALIFORNIA

I have a photograph of myself from when I was around 7 years old. I'm dressed up with all my dolls in the kitchen. One of my favorite dolls was the "Crissy Doll" (with hair that grew!). She was the tallest of my dolls and had long red hair. When you pushed a button on her back and pulled on her hair, her hair grew even longer. I loved playing with Crissy and having her interact with my other dolls. They were all my little friends. What I remember most about my Crissy Doll, was that one day, I got a hold of the scissors and gave her a very short hair cut. After that, Crissy's hair no longer grew. Most of my childhood memories are from photographs I've seen in the past, rather than actual memories. But I do remember how it felt to push that button on Crissy's back and let her hair grow.

I've been a "counter" for as long as I can remember. It started with the stairs in the home where I was raised. Even though I already knew there were 14 steps, I counted them each time I went up and down—it helped me feel safe. Sometimes, I would count anything in the house that had multiples: ceiling patterns, people in a room, lines on paper…The counting continued, and once I could spell words and learned to type, I would count the letters of different words and each letter by which hand typed it. Words that had the same number of letters on each side (when typed) were "feel good" words. Symmetry feels good to my brain and helps me feel safe inside my head.

My parents fought a lot as I grew up, and as a child, I believed it was somehow my fault. I believe my OCD tendencies were my way of trying to make things work out and help me feel safe in the midst of feeling anxious. At night in bed, I would say prayers—the same prayer each night—but then one night I added to my request to God to please bless each person in my family and my dog, Coco. If I left anyone out of this list, I was afraid something bad would happen to them.

As a child, I developed many self-soothing ways to feel safe. Most of them consisted of doing something a certain number of times or a certain way. This magical thinking was supposed to ensure that things went "right" or that nothing bad happened. If things didn't feel right, I thought maybe I should count the odd numbers, rather than even. It wasn't until I was well into adulthood that I learned to tell myself that this was not what caused accidents or bad things to happen. Still, somehow as a kid, I managed to feel that things were or would be my fault, especially if I didn't stay in control of my ritualistic habits.

The First Pull

As a teenager, the bathroom was one of the few places I could lock the door and be alone. We had one small bathroom in our three-bedroom house for the four of us. At some point, my mom changed the wallpaper to a 70's theme. The wallpaper was tan and black and had funny sayings, like "make love, not war" and "a bird in the hand can be messy, very," and some other spin-offs of popular, witty sayings of the 60's and 70's. Even though I had read them all before, each time I went to the bathroom, there they were—repeated all over the walls to be read again. It became a place of familiarity each time I sat down and reread them.

At some point when I was around 13 and in the midst of hormonal changes, I decided it was time to use Mom's tweezers to groom my bushy eyebrows. I'm not sure what happened that day, but I found myself spending a long time in front of the mirror each time I went into the bathroom. Me, the tweezers, and the mirror were like one. I was convinced that many of these eyebrow hairs were "bad hairs" that needed to be removed. I did so to the point that I had to pencil in my eyebrows. This was very embarrassing while in high school, since most girls at that time, including me, didn't yet wear eye makeup. I began to get a lot of strange looks and comments, mostly teasing about my funny eyebrows.

If I went anywhere near water, I couldn't go under and was afraid of getting my face wet for fear of losing my eyebrows and someone discovering that I didn't have too many. I tried to think up an excuse in case someone asked, but other than saying I got too close to the hot oven and they burned off, I couldn't think of a logical explanation. I didn't know why I had done this to myself and why I couldn't stop, and I didn't like looking different and being teased about it. This became more pronounced once I started dating, and I was afraid my eyebrows would be rubbed off if my face were touched. The bathroom could be a dangerous place. Even though it was my safe, familiar place, it became a place of hiding out and pulling out.

Sometime after my second semester in college, while home for a break, I pulled out a hair from my head. I don't remember what was going on that week, day, or moment. It just happened and it felt good—like the most natural, self-soothing thing I could do and had always done. Before long, I had to wear hats and bandanas in class and secretly bought my first wig from a random wig store in NYC on the way home on my next break.

It happened that this was the same place Liza Manelli had once gone to. I don't think I told the lady why I needed a wig, as I still didn't know yet what I had. I didn't tell my parents either, but Mom, who had been finding hair all over the wood floors for years, figured it out pretty fast.

And so began my long relationship with my once, long, beautiful hair. It was now my new obsession, vice and secret. I was too embarrassed to tell anyone that I pulled out my hair. I was sure I was the only person doing this and felt a lot of shame about it and the need to keep it hidden. I didn't tell my friends, and I didn't tell my boyfriends. I just tried to keep it hidden as best I could. This is how cutting my own hair started. Since I didn't want anyone to see what I'd done, I decided I would cut my own hair. Sometimes, this took a lot of time, since I had to cut it in such a way to cover up any thin or bald spots I had created. Sometimes, I got carried away with the scissors. I enjoyed the cutting feeling and obsessed over getting the cut just right. Usually, I ended up with a pretty decent looking hair cut and even got compliments occasionally. Sometimes, I didn't want anyone to know I had cut it myself.

Support

I think the first time I learned the term, "trichotillomania," was on the Internet, as I searched to understand what I had. It was then that I realized I had or did something that others did as well.

When I met my husband in my early 30's, I told him up front about my hair pulling. He had his own addictive tendencies and limitations and was very empathetic. Soon after, while living in Denver, I saw an ad in the paper for a trich support group for people who pulled out their hair. I was excited and scared to go to my first support meeting, but so grateful to know that I wasn't alone in having this crazy human condition. It was so wonderful to meet others who were just like me and understood what I was going through!

A few years later, with my husband's encouragement, I decided to go to an AA meeting to see if relating to trich as an addiction might help me be able to stop pulling. For a couple of years, I went to AA meetings, but told no one why I was there or that I wasn't an alcoholic. I actually would have been embarrassed to admit I pulled out my hair even in the midst of hearing so many difficult stories. The meetings did help me to refrain from pulling and the urges seemed to lessen. I decided to start a meeting for hair pullers using the 12-step model. I had spoken with some people who had done this for OCD, and I borrowed some of their material to start my own meeting.

Hair: More Hair and Less Hair

Some days, all it takes is waking up in the morning to feel like pulling my hair out. Every morning when I look in the mirror, I see "bad hairs." When I'm getting ready for work, brushing my hair in front of the bathroom mirror can be a setup for pulling. Hair brushing is something millions of people do every morning, which should only taken a couple of minutes, if that. But I see a hair in the mirror that is "different" from the others, and I feel instantly compelled to pull it out. I feel relieved. Then I see another "bad hair" and even though I know logically, "there's nothing wrong with this hair or the others," it's not convincing enough to stop me from taking the action to complete my desire.

When I'm already running late, being caught in the mirror does not help me to get out the door to work on time. This makes me feel more stress, because part of me wants to stop and go to work and part of me thinks I need to finish the search and pull, which could go on for quite a while. Finally, I am able to put my hat on and leave the bathroom. Sometimes, it only sets me back ten minutes, but I feel bad about myself afterwards.

Standing on a big rock in the sun, I see my shadow against the peach-colored paint of the house we've just moved into. I'm "rock climbing" with Munchkin, the younger of our two black cats. In the shadow image, I see my hand reach toward my head, as if in a salute to the hair that has just been set free.

Hairs Everywhere

I seem to have an extraordinary attention to detail. I notice things that may go overlooked by the majority of humans. Sometimes this feature is a useful trait that allows me to notice important things that can be very helpful. But when it comes to hair, this trait is more like a grooming mechanism gone awry. Strangely, (or maybe not), I notice hairs that appear—on people's clothes, a lost hair on the carpet, in my food (ich!), and just about wherever I go, I can't seem to get away from this noticing. Not a problem, right? Except that I have a visceral response to seeing these hairs, unless they are my own. Good thing I'm not a Chimpanzee!

When I let my fingers into my hair, they are on an instant "seek and destroy mission." The bad hairs represent everything from uncomfortable feelings to what I perceive as unacceptable parts of myself. I don't often want to be present and feel my feelings and this is usually when the pulling takes over, numbs me out, distracts me, and soothes me. But it leaves me depressed and frustrated to have both soothed and destroyed myself at my own hand. Sometimes I think it would be better to have been an alcoholic because there's so much more support.

I'm not sure if I've ever been 100% ready or committed to not pulling. I'm now 47. I've heard people say that trich doesn't define them, but for me, it's been such a huge part of my life, that it's difficult to relate to living without it. I've had many periods of little to no pulling, and did fine during those times, but it always comes back. Sometimes it feels like a shift in my being, where the pulling urges aren't there for awhile. Then they come back as if they were always a part of me. When I'm not pulling, my OCD tendencies usually get worst. Sometimes, it's easier to pull…it's a familiar friend, a place to go, where I know what to expect and have some control, albeit temporarily.

After many hours and years of pulling, my jaw, wrist, and shoulder muscles ache afterwards. If I've had a difficult spell of pulling, I often feel bad about myself. This affects my self-esteem, my ability to feel good about myself, to reach out and connect with others, and my willingness to do good things for myself. It affects my faith and connection with a Higher Power.

What was my worst moment with trich? Too many to choose from. Overall, this disorder/habit pattern has been a temporary reward with devastating effects. With all the work I've done and things I've tried and all the healing so far, I still feel that I have a long way to go. Sharing my story is a way to reach out to others who might be having a hard time with their pulling and know that they are not alone.

My best moments have been in times (usually of remission or support) where I've felt a level of compassion and self-empathy. The healing I've received has been from connecting with other pullers (especially in person) offering them empathy and support, knowing I'm not alone, and allowing myself to be accepted for who I am.

10
TIME TO TALK
SARAH, MID-TWENTIES, CANADA
CANADIAN BFRB SUPPORT NETWORK (CBSN),
FOUNDER

I started pulling my hair on the last day of Grade 7 when I was 13 years old. For some odd reason the older kids in my school had a strange tradition of having a massive "food fight" to celebrate the last day before summer. When I say food fight, I mean kids brought water balloons, shaving cream, eggs, toilet paper, ketchup and mustard, and water guns. I always enjoyed participating in this event because we would run around carefree and make a complete disaster of ourselves.

I went home that afternoon straight to the shower to clean out the mess of shaving cream, honey and other condiments that had formed a tiny home on top of my head. I remember while my hair was drying I found I had missed a part underneath that still had honey. I didn't want to get back in the shower, so I tried breaking it up with my fingers. This was the first time I accidentally pulled a few strands of hair out, and it was my first experience seeing a hair root. Initially I had no clue what it was, but it was interesting and I wanted to see more of it.

The next morning I woke up I suddenly remembered the new mysterious tip on my hair strand from the day before. That is where my battle with trich all started. I wasn't "enjoying" pulling my hair out—it hurt! But I was so determined to find another hair root and see it again. Slowly, but surely, I got better at getting one hair strand at a time and tugging on it just the right way, which allowed that glorious root to become free. It was fascinating to see!

For some reason, I began to bite the end off of the roots once I'd brought them to my lips. When I first started pulling it was mainly from my scalp. Today my scalp is the number one area, but I pull hair from everywhere EXCEPT eyelashes for some reason. I never got into that area. But I pull with tweezers from my eyebrows, arms, legs, pubic area and even armpits. Anywhere I can get a root.

I found myself looking for "roots" more frequently through the summer after Grade 7. I started to notice small patches of hair missing and panicked. What was I doing to myself?! There was no explanation for a 12 year old kid to pull out her hair. I had to tell my mom what I was doing; I was so embarrassed and felt ashamed of this weird habit I had developed. That's when my mom took me to the doctor. He explained some condition I couldn't even pronounce, let alone had ever heard of. He set up some appointments for me to meet with a child psychiatrist. Apparently this hair pulling thing—trichotillomania they called it—WAS heard of.

By the end of the summer I couldn't hide the patches. Some adults understood, most didn't care. I eventually became an easy target for some of the boys in my grade. A couple of them began to try and take my hat off and throw it around to each other until a teacher caught them, or one of my true friends got it back for me. I had to immediately cover my head with my arms and usually get something like a sweater or book to try and hide my head when this happened. I spent many days crying at lunch because of the teasing and (at the time I didn't know it) downright bullying.

I was sent to see a child psychiatrist to help with the trich. I had no idea what the hell I was doing there…what was he going to do to help solve my strange habit? Questions about my family life came up, my friends, my surroundings. I had never given much thought to my childhood and how it was, but up until that point I thought I had a pretty normal, GOOD childhood with all the love and attention I ever needed. The psychiatrist eventually put me on anti-depressants, with my parents' permission of course, because there was a two percent chance they would help me overcome this disorder. *It's worth a shot*, my parents and I thought.

I continued pulling more and more through the fall of that year, causing more harm to my head and creating more bald spots. This psychiatrist really attempted to get me into deep conversations about my relationship with my family. Other than giving me minor tips such as wearing a hat, cutting my nails short, snapping a rubber band when I feel the urge to pull, I wasn't getting anywhere with this guy. My parents were getting frustrated more and more because I was having breakdowns pretty much every day at home about how crappy I felt and looked. I had gained weight from not being able to participate in swimming and other activities I used to feel confident about, and I'm sure puberty didn't help.

I was halfway through the school year, it was spring, and I was still pulling and wearing a hat. My anti-depressant dosage had been raised several times because there was zero improvement while I'd taken them over a few months. I had my close friends at school that stuck by me and didn't change, but I had lost so many people who I considered friends. I was officially an outcast at school. I had always been on the more "popular" side of the schoolyard... sporty, confident, and had been the target of many boys' crushes. Grade 8 and the lack of hair suddenly took all of that away from me. I continued to gain weight (partially due to the antidepressants) and lose confidence. I still continued seeing my psychiatrist on a regular basis but found it very unhelpful. I felt like he was looking for something I couldn't give him, mostly an explanation as to what was wrong with me. I just didn't know.

The dosage on my antidepressant (PAXIL at the time) was so high I began to behave... strangely. I had bursts of anger, I was physically abusive towards my mom, and constant crying and screaming were the sounds coming from my house. One night I had a fit and my nose began to bleed really badly. It wouldn't stop, but for some reason I was so angry at my mom and sister and just so out of it. My sister drove my mom and me to the emergency room where I was given a sedative.

Turns out I was overdosing on PAXIL. The dosage prescribed to me was considered dangerously high for a full grown adult, let alone a 12 year old kid. I let my mom deal with the doctors and the adult stuff. All I knew was that I was being asked by a new child psychiatrist if I would like to be given a chance to stay at a youth medical facility where I would be monitored and properly given medication suited for me, and get some therapy for the hair pulling. Of course I wanted help. So I said yes. And that's when I was taken to a psychiatric children's ward at a hospital. I didn't know this at the time of course. All I knew is that it was a bit strange that I wasn't allowed to leave the floor, not allowed to wear shoelaces, or keep pens in my room. I was there a whole week, a week away from home and the screaming, the bullies at school, and reality. I was 14 and hated everything I knew, including myself. This was definitely my worst moment around trich.

I graduated elementary school, and by this point I was happy to get the hell away from all these kids who I thought were my friends but had become these assholes (to put it nicely). I was free. Summer had come, and I would be going to an all girls' high school that September with a few girl friends. During the summer, I worked hard on my hair pulling. I created a countdown on MSN messenger that kept track of everyday I didn't pull. I didn't pull all summer. I still had patches that prohibited me from going swimming, wearing my hair down, etc, but I got used to wearing a hat or bandana. I was finally free of antidepressants, and I stopped seeing the therapist after the hospital incident. I was doing okay on my own. I did my own research online and found new tricks to help me stop, along with resources that showed me I wasn't the only one out there with this strange disorder called trichotillomania.

Prior to the first day of high school, my mom took me to meet the principal to explain my condition, and that I would be wearing a hat/bandana. She was an amazingly supportive woman, and I appreciated her kindness. This was going to be a good place for me. I felt it.

When I went into Grade 9 I was often asked why I was allowed to wear a hat, and I always replied with "I have a medical condition." That was that. Nobody bothered me, only a few times teachers would stop and say, "take your hat off young lady," but I just showed them the principal's note I carried around in my knapsack that gave me permission. I was still not pulling, and my hair was growing back. I finally felt myself around my newfound friends in the school. It was a safe place.

After that first year of high school, I had been pull free for over a year. That summer going into Grade 10, I got a haircut. It was short, not the greatest look for me, but I had hair. I didn't have to wear a hat for the first time in two years. It felt amazing. I promised myself I would appreciate my hair, I would do it every day and take the time to really appreciate the fact I could style it and go out in public feeling normal.

The first day of Grade 10 was AMAZING. Everyone couldn't believe I wasn't wearing a hat. It was a great year and I had several pull-free years following it. I had been able to overcome trichotillomania (or so I thought for many years)! I did have the occasional slip up where I would pull one or two hairs, but it didn't affect me. Slowly but surely I was confident again, felt good about my looks, and had dyed my hair several different colours to figure out what my style was.

Being 24 now, I have had so much happen in between my first major pulling episode and now. I went to university for Social Work. I was doing great until my dad died in March of 2010. That was the beginning of my new downward spiral. I finished third year of university completely numb, fell into a severe deep depression that summer, and barely graduated fourth year. My severe depression was the worst experience of my entire life. It was so painful, and lasted so long. I could not work, and my relationships were put through hell and back. I wanted to die. Even through all of this, I hadn't pulled to the point of having visible bald spots, but for some reason, the stress of trying to find a full time job, and a couple of rough patches with external factors, I started pulling again.

Here I am today, exactly 10 years after my first pulling episode. This disorder is so mysterious, and I have had hid the fact I have trichotillomania from people for many years. Not anymore. This round, I will educate people along the way. I will reduce the stigma attached with this disorder and other mental health issues. People reacting in a negative way because they think it is just so bizarre or "disgusting" to them. I tend to not care anymore about what people think.

It's time to talk about trich. The power of several voices is what will help break the stigma. It's about time for BFRBs to get the necessary attention in the medical field it deserves. It affects so many people, and to not talk about it doesn't help. I am pretty fed up with the lying and the pretending that this disorder doesn't affect my life in such a huge way. It controls my life to some degree, and if we all stay silent, it will continue to sit on the back burner of the mental health system. We deserve answers, as do our parents.

As I mentioned before, I stopped pulling for 10 years, and I stopped by using a countdown method of counting how many days I went without pulling. I kept track by using social media (msn messenger at the time). I think I reached my breaking point of feeling like total crap, and it used sheer willpower. Wearing my hat at home does help me. I pull only at home, so having the hat on is a barrier, until I decide to take it off of course. Not having greasy hair also helps. I wash my hair everyday. I think also speaking with someone about it when I have a rough day is extremely beneficial. You need to have an outlet when you have all these emotions bottled up, so I recommend a journal of some sort. Whether it's a personal diary, or a more public version online. Talking about it is a truly soothing/healing way to deal with a BFRB.

*You can contact me on Twitter: @skrobertson89 or www.canadianbfrb.org.

11

A LONG LIFE PULLING
JOSÉ, LATE FIFTIES, SPAIN

Accordling to my knowledge of trichotillomania (TTM), I always thought that it was important to take corrective steps from the age of onset. I also believed that an early onset, even without treatment, would provide better prognosis. In 2010, I read an article on TTM[1]. After reading it, I came to the conclusion that the age of onset does not make much difference. That is, there are no children under six years old *"very early onset, (veo),"* that tend to correct themselves, as I believed. On the contrary, according Flessner et al. an early beginning can lead to a long life of pulling. Could there be a direct relationship between very early onset and chronicity?

I am now 57 years old, and I started pulling out my hair when I was 3 years old. This is my story. I am a teacher of children with Special Educational Needs and a psychologist. I have a daughter and two sons, 30, 28 and 26 years old respectively. I have had TTM for approximately 40 years.

I would describe TTM as a need to pull out one's hair coupled with feelings of anxiety. In moments of stress or tension I pull my hair as a way of overcoming the anxiety. Pulling brings comfort and the relief. I have failed repeatedly to resist the strong impulse of TTM.

---

[1] Flessner, CA, Lochner, C, Stein, DJ, Woods, DW, Franklin, ME, & Keuthen, NJ (2010). "Age of Onset of Trichotillomania Symptoms: Investigating Clinical Correlates." *J Nerv Ment Dis*. Dec; 198 (12):896-900

I have not had any medical illness related to this and have always had beautiful hair that I pulled out even when I was with my friends, my children, and my family. I knew that I could not continue that way."

When I was five years old my family began to give my TTM some attention. My mother did not know what to do and tried all types of things to stop me. After awhile it was too much. As my TTM increased during childhood, the whole family came to see where and how big my bald patches were. Between the ages of eight and twelve, I often went to school with my fingers bound with sticking plaster so that I could not grip my hair. But I had a trick. Only the fingers of my left hand were bound because I had to write with my right. Whenever I could, I discarded the pen that I had in my right hand, and I was still able to pull my hair, again and again.

I tried to disguise the problem by wearing a traditional cap or putting black makeup on the bald patches to hide them. My mother decided that the solution was to have my head shaved, which made my friends, family, and all people in the neighbourhood jeer. The suffering was terrible. When I went to the hairdresser and the barber cut my hair off, I felt even worse seeing his satisfied expression. I imagined him with the same haircut to make myself feel a little better. The barber wore a wide smile as he shook my hair from his apron onto the floor, as if he understood the reason for my baldness. When I left the hairdresser I didn't know where to hide. I stayed at home the rest of that day because I was so embarrassed.

The nicknames I received were varied. "The Calvi" was popular, which in Spanish means, "the bald one." I was also called "The Three Hair." I do not remember them all, but I am sure that the nicknames could have filled many pages.

When relatives came to see me, it turned into an awful experience for a misunderstood child. My personal image crumbled as my self-esteem deteriorated to the point of not wanting to be recognized in pictures, photos or videos. There was a permanent tension and a struggle to conceal the effects of my TTM.

In 2005, Dra. Christine Lochner said that there were "similarities between OCD and TTM, which have been widely recognized; but at the same time there is evidence of important differences between these two disorders."[2] Actually the TTM is included in DSM V within a category of

---

[2] Christine Lochner, Ch, Seedat, S, Pieter L du Toit, Daniel G Nel Niehaus, Dana JH Sandler, R. & Stein, DJ. (2005): "Obsessive-compulsive disorder and trichotillomania: a phenomenological comparison." *BMC Psychiatry 2005*, 5:2.

Obsessive-Compulsive and Related Disorders.

In 1989, Dra. Susan Swedo described the first cases of sudden onset of OCD in children who have undergone a strep infection.[3] In these cases, the condition is defined as Pediatric Autoimmune Neuropsychiatric disease associated with Streptococcus (PANDAS) and the symptoms are similar to those suffering from obsessive-compulsive disorder, but little is said about the TTM.

I had strep throat at four years old. I do not know if this might've played a role in triggering the TTM because for much of my childhood I was sick and feverish with tonsillitis until I had surgery to have my tonsils removed. I also had to endure an alcoholic grandfather as a child. He was a good person whom I loved very much, but he caused much suffering in the family.

Nobody in Spain in that time (1960-1970) knew that the wearing of caps, the colouring of the bald patches or the use of adhesive bandages, were strategies to attempt to change my behaviour.

My mother said to me that I had to go out and not stay at home all the time. In time I married and had children but the problem did not decrease. When I reached my thirties, I intended to look for professional help and I found a good psychologist. The psychologist's work followed the pattern of humanistic psychology. He helped me to solve the problem.

There was a significant remission of pulling, and I thought that I had eliminated the problem forever. But I had not. It returned again when my mother got Alzheimer's. Alzheimer's can bring the worst out of anything and anyone.

Stress is not always considered cause of TTM, but in my case I think it was. My mother suffered from post-traumatic stress after my father died (he had an accident at work in 1956); at that time I was six months old. I was separated from my mother for a brief time and looked after by another woman. I grew up as an only son with my maternal grandparents who were like my own parents. I was much loved, and I had very good social support from my father's family as well.

---

[3] Swedo Se, Rapoport JL, Cheslow DL, Leonard HL, Ayoub EM, Hosier DM et al. "High prevalence of obsessive-compulsive symptoms in patients with Sydenham's chorea." *Am J Psychiatry 1989*; 146: 246 -249.

After finishing some courses of Transactional Analysis, I decided to go to the university, and I got a degree in psychology. I have always been a scalp puller. Over the years, my pulling has produced balding patches on the crown of my head and some on both sides. Nevertheless, I can say now I have been free from pulling for more than ten years.

My TTM has not prevented me from having a normal life. I have a good family, a good job and some hobbies. I am more or less happy, and I help people with TTM.

I had to look after my mother and to take care of her Alzheimer's for nine years. She died after ten years and it was then that my hair pulling problem occurred again.

At this point I am free and it is now when I have to face the small relapses.

I have not had any problems of health. I have not taken any type of medication to solve the problem. I have never had problems with my joints, like other people that I know. My fingers are not swollen and I do not have much tightness in my back. Despite having a long time pulling, the TTM has not created any general health problems.

The treatment based on Transactional Analysis had not been completely positive. I have more than 10 years of remission and continue to overcome the urge, but I have not eliminated it completely. Relapses took place because of a situation of stress.

At the moment I am free from the problem, due to the application of self-treatment more than ten years ago. It was based on the pattern of cognitive-behaviour and I hope to continue this way.

The treatment was for a trichotillomania chronicle and here is the abstract:

This work presents a treatment of chronic trichotillomania. It looked to differentiate which components of the treatment based on behavioral techniques such as habit reversal are the most important and significant and therefore more effective for their simplification and cost reduction in the clinic and how the self-evaluation could eliminate it. It is carried out through self-treatment by the author of this work and following Llavona & Carrasco, (1985) in the establishment of the two phases of their work. Male 43 years old pulling his hair out more than 40 years, with 10 of remission. The rest of the remissions have been very fluctuating, short and without solution. The training is applied in the competition reaction –habit reversal-, and self-monitoring, together with the relaxation and visualization, in a first phase. It was not necessary to apply the second phase consistent in the application of stimulus control, massed practice and self-control. After the first phase of 13 weeks, the behavior problems disappeared and did not occur in the next 4 months at the end of the treatment.

Key words: TRICHOTILLOMANÍA, TRAINING IN COMPETITION REACTION, SELF-EVALUATION & SEL-MONITORING, HABIT REVERSAL.
It is published here in
Spanish: www.psicologiacientifica.com/tricotilomania-tratamiento-conductal/

Relapses occur when we do not expect them. Stressful events can distort our life, and in my case, cause episodes of hair pulling. However, it depends on how we think about it.

If we face the relapses as a challenge, we will have the resources to confront and learn from them in the future. If we see them as compromises to our integrity and safety, we will most probably deteriorate. Happiness rests in being firmly secure and keeing our eyes open for those moments that make us feel thankful for all we have.

We have to know that TTM produces social shame, recurrences, and in many cases, chronicity. Because of this, we need information and to learn about the problem if we want to manage it well.

Throughout my long life of hair pulling I have learned several things. Here are some of them:

- Identify the triggers.
- Acknowledge the problem, but no more than that.
- Express our emotions.
- Have friends, hobbies, and exercise. Help people if we have free time.
- Listen actively. To feel listened to and understood makes us feel better about ourselves and others.
- Do something for others. Selflessly helping others is a great source of satisfaction. Let us stop being the center of the world, relativize the TTM, and learn how to be less selfish and more tolerant. Getting into another's skin of enriches us by an experience of

93

shared humanity. It opens up new perspectives to analyze and solves one's own problems. The TTM is not the center of our lives.

- Be positive. Personal happiness and fulfillment in relationships do not depend on what happens, but how we live and experience what happens to us. Any circumstances always hides positive things including our TTM, why not?
- Listen to your emotions. Emotions offer valuable clues to knowing ourselves. Do not be too demanding on yourself.
- Be gracious as you would be with your best friend. And of course ask for professional help if you need it. Do not be lazy, the sooner the better.
- Nobody is perfect and you are not the only person in the world. Relax. Nothing and nobody will sink because you made a mistake or pulled out your hair.

At present I have a website in Spanish and coordinate a mailing list on Yahoo for people with TTM. If you want to contact me, I would like to share and write about our experiences with TTM. I have suffered a lot, but I am pull free now. We will be able to share emotions, frustrations, and why not our successes, too?

*I can be emailed at: ttmania09@yahoo.es. I can also be found on es.groups.yahoo.com/neo/groups/tricotilomaniaorg/info, or blogging at www.tricotilomania.org

12 *TRICH: IT'S JUST A THING*
DIANA, LATE FORTIES, CANADA

I write this in my 48th year. Over the years, through trial and error I found ways to keep my problem very minimal. Excepting the Wig Years and the summer of 2012, most of my life it has been under reasonable control. So, in all I've had 36 years of mostly containable trich with two major episodes. The first episode was so traumatic it affected me permanently. Let's just say I'm glad I come from the pre-social media era, or I might not be here to write this, given my adolescence.

Although any actual pulling has been very minimal for over a year now, you wouldn't know it to look at me. I have a comparatively mild case. Even so I haven't been able to leave the house without something covering my head for several years now. My main area is the upper back crown of my head where I have a double whorl and ironically, a biopsy scar from when I was tested for Alopecia. It starts there and then widens into a circle on top, like Friar Tuck. I also favour the area around my right ear for some reason. After such a long time of favouring a particular spot, the regrowth is sporadic at best. I imagine the follicles have scar tissue. It is sparse, bristly and transparent. There is some white regrowth there, and I'm hoping it will continue.

Last summer was exceptional. By the end of it, I looked like Sméagol. That year was a stressful one. Last July I was summoned for jury duty, and I also needed to have my photo ID renewed, both in the same week. Of all the worst possible times! Purchasing a wig for myself was like revisiting a battlefield. Oh, the irony of a wearing a wig for identification purposes! Trying to put it on made me nauseous. I'd stand there, hand on my outthrust hip, making snide remarks like a catty crossdresser, "Who do you think you are?"… "Get off my corner, honey!" … "You're not fooling anyone." I literally couldn't force myself to walk out the door wearing it. One morning I danced the Cucaracha on it before forcefully kicking it behind the toilet.

I recently had partial weft and partial clip extensions put in. This evens out and blends the irregular lengths as it grows back, which it does with all the vigour and velocity of a hundred-year tortoise. However, I still have to cover the topmost back of my head in the meantime.

I have a teenage daughter. There are hundreds of pictures of her and her friends at every stage of development. All her dances, concerts, and days at the beach. The ubiquitous duckface selfies. Of course, she asked about mine, wondering why she'd never seen them. Although I owned the very same model of Polaroid camera used today as the Instagram logo, there is no photographic evidence of my teenage years.

I remember a picnic with my dad when I was about twelve. He was extracting inner blades of grass from their outer sheath and biting the white bulb off the end. I started doing the same thing and it was pleasantly absorbing, sitting in the sun nibbling grass roots with Dad. At some point shortly before Grade 8, in a repeat performance of this innocent pastime, I managed to accidentally pick out almost all of my eyebrows. Just in time to sit in the front row for picture day.

I needed to have an electroencephalogram the same year, which required conductive gel applied to my scalp to attach the wires. I still had the gunk in my hair afterward, and I could feel it shriveling up as it dried. The sensation was creepy—in a good way. I was picking it off the way kids will peel dried Elmer's glue off their hands. I could still feel it in there after I had shampooed it. I was never quite the same after, like I had become ultra-conscious of my scalp.

When I first started high school, at a regular public school, I got into the habit of falling asleep with several partially read books piled up around me. I would often read until two or three in the morning. I would wake up with little mouse-nests of hair beside me; hairs stuck between pages of books, and not consciously remember plucking my head in the night.

By the end of the school year I could no longer hide it. The family doctor referred me to a dermatologist. He took a punch biopsy, and I was given a prescription for cortisone cream and told to come in monthly for cortisone injections to the scalp. The diagnosis was Alopecia Areata, and I wasn't about to argue.

I did NOT tell my parents I was responsible for it. How would I even begin? It was already like a sin of omission with the Alopecia diagnosis. How could I backpedal from that and drop a bombshell? This was 1978. Trichotillomania wasn't a recognized condition until 1987. A mental hospital or a child protection investigation was a real possibility. I was afflicted with something that didn't yet exist.

The Wig Years

Over the March break my mother took me to a fancy ladies' wig shop. This was the age of classic rock, Chevy vans and the natural look. I might have had easier time finding a wig if I'd naturally had short, straight brown hair with bangs. But we sought a prosthetic replacement for my formerly enviable head of thick, soft, dark blonde hair. The closest match they had was a waist-long synthetic full-cap in a lighter, golden shade. I looked like a cartoon princess until we had it cut to look somewhat more realistic, however, the part and hairline were still painfully obvious. I didn't enjoy experimenting with hairstyles and makeup, so the wig wore me. I felt absolutely humiliated—as if I were wearing a dunce's cap or a scarlet letter. I also felt guilty because of how much it had cost.

In retrospect, I guess it seemed phony and pretentious for my quiet, sardonic and agile self. No matter which way I tried to style the wig, it lent a certain "dumb blonde" element to my persona like over-the-top glam makeup or obvious breast implants might have. I felt like a porn actress. We called the wig "Big Bertha," and Mom called its' Styrofoam stand, "Teenage Head." I was already something of an oddball, but when I had to start wearing an obvious synthetic hairpiece, the social ostracism reached new heights. Kids at school called me "Miss Wiggy," although a few of the more sensitive ones asked if I had cancer. Most thought it was some kind of ridiculous affectation on my part.

Getting ready to go anywhere became a time-sucking chore and my dad would make inane comments about the vanity of teenage girls and the amount of time women spend in bathrooms.

Oh, did I mention I don't like wigs?

When I look back I taste fear. I felt that this habit could get me in very serious trouble beyond the scope of my comprehension. I worried that it was a symptom, just the early signs of something worse developing. I used to sneak books about abnormal psychology into bed and read with a flashlight under the covers in an attempt to find out. Was I developing some kind unnatural perversion, along the lines of necrophilia? Some form of psychosis? Was it something supernatural, even? I was petrified of being sent to some austere, dormitory-style juvenile detention asylum with bunk beds, group therapy and a matron. I'd never so much as shared a room with a sibling.

I went to regular public school up until Grade 10, when my mother fortuitously discovered a different kind of school that didn't require daily classroom attendance. I was able to do most of my assignments at home and only needed go to the brick-and-mortar building once a week. Not knowing what to expect from the future, I leapt at the chance to own a small business, even before I was officially out of my teens.

My parents were as supportive as they knew how to be at the time. For all intents and purposes, I was considered to have Alopecia. It seemed to take my parents a long time to really realize the extent of harassment I dealt with at the public school in Grade 9. That wig certainly wasn't making me any friends. They figured most people would be reasonable and kind and the wig would help me fit in and feel less self-conscious.

At one point in school my wig was yanked off my head in the jostling hallway, tossed around like a football and shoved into a locker. I didn't have a circle of friends to step in and help, it was a huge big-city school, and I was something of a loner. I didn't even know the kids that did it. It was probably done on a dare.

Sometimes full-on panic attacks happened, trying to get out the door. We lived in a high-rise condo. Getting on the elevator was only the beginning of a series of dizzyingly embarrassing entrances for me. Mustering up the courage to go the through one door was exhausting. What fresh hell lurked behind the next one? By the time I got to my desk (if I made it that far) I had repeated this "doors of perception" routine half a dozen times.

If an elevator came and there were people in it, I'd often decline and take my chances on the next one. I couldn't stand having people looking at me in close proximity. Windy subway tunnels and jam-packed trains were a whole new level of horror. The cafeteria was just unthinkable. I ate my lunch in a stall in the washroom. If I heard other girls in there, I would wait until the coast was clear before emerging, rather than be stuck in front of the mirrors wondering if I dared attempt to brush my "hair" in case it came off in the sink. The school I went to had girls that would beat you up if they made a comment and you talked back to them. No way could I risk having that wig pulled off again.

School authorities perceived my inexplicable absences as delinquent behaviour. I was considered a particularly stubborn serial truant because I was frequently late. So often that sometimes it was more expedient to just call in sick and avoid interrupting a class in session, going to the principal's office, and facing a detention. Attending the detentions was difficult as I could hardly bear to enter the damned school in the first place.

I was told things like, "There are rude people, some ignorant kids will tease… That's an unfortunate pat of life. They're everywhere. Just ignore it. People grow out of it. As an adult you'll see that most are too preoccupied with their own problems to be judging others." Sound advice, but it didn't change what was happening right then. It didn't serve to punish the perpetrators, preserve my dignity, or assuage my anger.

It is obvious to me now, in retrospect that I was dealing with not just the trich but social phobia, and I often wonder chicken-or-egg fashion, which came first. It's hard to imagine these days with all the media attention given to bullying, that this would be so completely overlooked, but it was. At some point just toward the end of the school year, school authorities conceded to let me study outside of the classroom setting, and I was provided a private room near the Principal's office.

I had gossip and rumours spread about me. In an attempt at humour, my phone number posted on bathroom walls, along with the phrase, "for a good time, call Miss Wiggy." Strangers called the house at all hours of the night, and the irony was lost on my overprotective father, especially at 3 a.m.

As I got older, with some ingenuity we found practical workarounds, like alternative school and self-employment. I was able to get little jobs in offices doing clerical tasks. Then, in a brilliant stroke of luck, my boyfriend at the time and I were given the opportunity to own and operate a favourite store together, which friends of ours were selling. We jumped at the chance, and that went well for four or five years. During the first year with the shop my hair grew back entirely. Eventually we sold it and went our separate ways. I was again on the job market.

Having gone straight into the workforce from high school, I'd postponed college, and as a result did not yet qualify for anything more ambitious than data entry. Although by then I had a full head of hair, I hadn't bargained on being completely unable to look people in the eye, which caused me to be perceived as dishonest. This in turn caused employers to keep an extra-careful eye on me, which was exactly what I was afraid of. My alternative lifestyle with my shop had been so insular that I hadn't actually noticed any impairment until I was actually confronted with these situations.

As a young woman, I really took this little chestnut of social etiquette personally, "Your hair is the first thing people see and they form an opinion about you in the first 30 seconds." There's nothing like that to inspire confidence at your next interview.

In the early 1990s, I saw the T-word mentioned in a letter to Ann Landers. I immediately made the connection. At the end of the article, she gave out the address of The Trichotillomania Leaning Centre in California. I wrote away for more information, which they immediately sent. I informed TLC that I had only discussed trich a few times over the years with the occasional doctor, who always seemed to be searching for childhood trauma. As for childhood trauma, I had a fairly pleasant, uneventful childhood with loving, mild-mannered parents in a comfortable middle class home. I did print extra copies of a rudimentary self-monitoring worksheet that TLC provided. The medication I briefly tried was called Clomipramine. It was like prescribing Thorazine for a cold. Within a couple of days I was drooling uncontrollably and sleeping all the time. For the few hours I was awake I shambled around like a zombie and my vision was blurred. Needless to say, I couldn't go to work in this condition. A couple of sick days like that can add up to not earning enough for rent that month. Obviously, I discontinued the treatment.

I was eventually able to work as a secretary and go to college part time. I did this through temporary employment agencies. This got around the problem of my terror over interviews and the constant threat of being fired. I have had employers and coworkers speculate that I might be a closet alcoholic because of the pattern of absenteeism/tardiness. Despite the fact that I'm conscientious to a fault, I was at best perceived as an unreliable flake. I accepted what were probably illegal terminations because it was just too complicated and embarrassing to explain.

I don't have the financial security I should have at my age, and I worry about how I will survive in retirement. I have lost many income earning years, and have usually had to settle for low paying jobs that didn't have a company pension or benefit package. The rest of the time I was either self-employed or a stay-at-home mother. I am now doing medical transcription at home. I don't have retirement savings and home ownership remains out of reach.

I'd have to say the worst part about having trichotillomania is the stigma. To the uninitiated, the word Trichotillomania suggests major mental illness. The average Joe doesn't read Latin. You know, like there's Schizophrenia, and then there's Paranoid Schizophrenia... this is Tricho-tillo-mania! The psychiatric stigma reminds me of that "Gay Jerry" Seinfeld episode... "Not that there's anything wrong with it if I was, but I'm NOT mentally ill!"

There is so much erroneous, subjective and outdated information out there. A cursory search brings up results like "Trichotillomania is a mental disorder, along with pyromania, kleptomania and compulsive gambling... traumatic incident...blah blah...effectively treated with psychotherapy and medications."

In actual practice, few of us find that to be relevant. I don't believe this condition is psychological in nature. I wonder about the blanket acceptance of that theory, when in real life, there is very little evidence to support this. It's that nobody questions it or talks back. I don't say this as a newcomer in denial. I say this as a lifetime veteran who has seen trends and theories come and go. I really think it has to do with central nervous system and not the mind. I think it has to do with sensory processing, touch and texture.

Genuinely useful research seems to be lagging behind without any real progress being made in a decades. While awareness is on the increase, it only results in people feeling a sense of relief and kinship knowing others are out there with the same "psychiatric disorder," but doesn't challenge the assumption that it is one in the first place.

Trich in My Own Words

It is a frustrating burden and a pain in the ass. It started as a comfortable, mindless habit—like rubbing your chin while contemplating, or absentmindedly chewing the end of your pencil. But, it has an element to it that is like... movie theatre popcorn. It is nearly impossible to stop. Who has just one kernel? You have to finish it! And I find the rough, crispy regrowth texture of my hair to be unbearably enticing. For me to get a pixie cut or shave my head would be courting disaster. This would be innocuous enough, but it quickly becomes disfiguring as it progresses.

You'd think the disfigurement would be a pretty strong deterrent. Yes, and you'd thing the blistering and bleeding would be a pretty strong deterrent for those weak-willed souls who insist on scratching at their chicken pox and poison ivy, too.

The word "pulling" sounds too drastic or aggressive to describe it because it isn't a painful, handful-grasping, masochistic thing. It isn't intentionally self-destructive. It's satisfying in the same way potato chips have "that satisfying crunch." It's a pleasant sensation, like a good thorough back scratch. I'd also describe it as daydreaming, thinking, or concentrating. I've seen this described as a trance and have been asked about that by doctors. I think this is another example of too much clinical weight being placed on common vernacular descriptions. It's easily misunderstood as a dissociative state. I think there have been some mistakes made on the part of therapists taking patients' colloquial anecdotes literally.

Once I've pulled the hair, I bite off the root and chew it into tiny pieces. Getting the root is the sole reason that I pull. Sometimes I jab myself underneath my lower lip with the rooted tips first. It is not about the hair or the pulling at all; it's all about extracting that root. It's like getting a sunflower kernel out of the shell with the tip of your tongue and always digging through the package looking for a bigger, crunchier seed.

I've used neutral toned scarves and bandanas to try and hide the effects of trich. Frankly, I'm offended by well-intentioned suggestions like, "You should get a wig. It would make you feel more normal." (Insert gales of derisive laughter.) I'd like to say, "If I were to wear a wig it would make YOU more comfortable around me, and furthermore why are you suggesting I should feel bad?"

I'm relatively open about my trich and will talk about it on a need-to-know basis. If I am directly asked, I just say I have a medical condition. The ball is in their court to pursue the matter further. I really dislike the psychiatric stigma.

I can't say I really relate to triggers. It's not about stress. Nothing in particular brings on the pulling. I notice the urges increase around PMS, being overtired and possibly certain foods, commercial peanut butter in particular.

Things that don't help me include attempting to exercise willpower. Short hair. Psychotherapy. Medications. The 12-step model. Journal-keeping. Jargon and slogans. Stress balls, fidget toys. Busywork for its own sake. Someone monitoring, reminding me or touching my hands. As you might imagine, I won't wear a wig!

Finding a way to at least manage and contain trich is an individual process of trial and error. What seems to work in the meantime is an individualized compilation of best practices. I like to remind myself "that's not necessary" or "let it grow" rather than, "stop pulling" or "don't pull."

I don't rely on willpower. This whole abstinence-based recovery concept seems to be a new trend. I had never heard of it until I joined an Internet support board and saw hundreds of people struggling to stop this chronic condition using willpower. Failing, getting back up, and counting the days...It made me think of yo-yo dieting and the despair was palpable. I don't consider myself to be battling, struggling with, suffering from, or a victim of this. I'm living with a condition that science doesn't yet understand. I suspect it is neurological rather than psychological.

Sunflower seeds satisfy the need to bite, and I have a rubber scalp massage brush that provides a good facsimile of the scalp sensation. I also like to knit sometimes, when I'm actually making something. Then it's "just one more row..." If the urges are especially bad I'll resort to wearing a hairnet or putting a hot-oil treatment on my hair.

I am somewhat active in the support group and toss in my few cents here and there with anecdotes and bits of advice that have helped me. In turn, the mere fact that I'm ON a support board helps keep me accountable.

I like to think more in terms of prevention and damage control. I think that's more realistic. Forget groping in the dark for a possible cause, analysing your trich inside out and backwards trying to find reason and meaning. Just deal with the now. At the end of the day, it's just a thing. We've all got one.

13
CHANGING THE WORLD ONE HEAD AT A TIME
CHRISTINA, EARLY THIRTIES, NEW JERSEY

I have no recollection of feeling that very first hair plucked from its safe little hiding place in my scalp. There is no specific moment that made me grab a hair (or two, or ten) and yank with all of my strength just so I could see, and most likely, ingest the bulb on the end of it. I was only nine years old when I became a "trichster."

It was the summer before I was to enter fourth grade. I was to return to the Catholic school I had attended since first grade because my parents wanted me to be a "well-rounded" individual, deeply rooted in manners and discipline beyond the comprehension of any child my age. The issue was that I was TERRIFIED of my soon-to-be teacher. My older brother, and only sibling, was her student two years prior. My brother, Matt, a straight A student like me, had less than pleasant things to say about her. He never said she was a bad teacher, or that she was mean; on the contrary he implied how incredibly tough and strict she was. My internal panic button was set to overdrive at this point.

I have always only pulled from my scalp. Even now, at 33, when I get my eyebrows waxed, the pain of having my hair yanked from anywhere other than my scalp hurts so badly I tear up like a two year old who just had their lollipop fall on the ground. I have always had a pattern to my pulling.

I started in the left front of my bangs area and worked my way around to the right side, paying close attention the area near my ears. Once I reached the right side, my pulling would subside until the next personal tragedy would strike, and my scalp would consequently suffer. I would almost always eat the root of my hair and had a severe fixation with the red tipped ones. They were the crunchiest ones and gave me the ultimate satisfaction when I ground them to smithereens in between my front teeth.

I have also been obsessed with the "different" hairs: the wiry, Velcro ones, the gray ones, the ones that stood straight up when the rest of my hair was slicked back into a neat little ponytail, the super thick ones, the random red ones mingled in a forest of dark brown ones.

When my first bald patch appeared, my mother did what any normal parent would do. She demanded an explanation, and like most trichsters I know, I denied all of it. I played stupid. I knew why my hair was missing, but I sure as hell wasn't going to tell her why. She took me to a dermatologist, who immediately told my mom and I it was most likely a disorder known as Alopecia causing my baldness, but he wanted to take a plug of my scalp just to be sure. At that very moment I thought that I could no longer hide the truth. You can imagine my surprise when the doctor called two weeks later to *confirm* my diagnosis of Alopecia, thus ending my trust that doctors could help me with my hair pulling.

Fast forward a few years and I was in the same school, in sixth grade. Now, of course, there were 22 students in my class, and at least 15 of them were little assholes. My pulling had become so severe that my parents were generous enough to buy me a wig. (Although in retrospect, I am not sure whether or not their embarrassment was a factor in this purchase.) Picture a nice, warm day in spring. The class was fortunate enough to go outside after lunch because of the gorgeous weather. I was walking in the field, talking to my girlfriends and passed two boys, David and Chris, who thought it hilarious if they ripped my wig right off of my head. So they did, and then proceeded to play "Monkey in the Middle" with it. I was completely exposed to every student, teacher, and nun in that school. I don't remember running to the bathroom. But I do remember the two girls who brought it to me, and I am still friends with them to this day, and have never, EVER, worn a wig since.

I recall exactly how difficult it was to grow up with trich. My older brother, in a desperate attempt to be Mr. Cool, chimed in when his "friends" called me "Baldilocks and the Three Hairs," or "Rocky and Baldwinkle." I remember being 9 years old, walking home in my Catholic school uniform, complete with the plaid jumper, painfully itchy sweater vest, and those awful saddle shoes. But my most vivid memory of walking home from grade school is walking home *alone*. Because my brother was too embarrassed to be seen with me, he made me linger behind him a block or two. I cried on an almost daily basis because all I ever wanted to do was walk home next to him, even if it was just once.

Of my parents, my mom was most definitely the more supportive of the two. She was the one who carted me from doctor to doctor, shrink to shrink, desperately seeking help for her daughter. She was the one who took me to get my wig. She was the one who took some fabric after the seamstress hemmed my prom gown and covered a plastic headband so I had something to wear in my hair. She took it a step further, and even had the florist attach some baby's breath to it, in loving attempt to make me *think* that my hair looked a little better than usual. My mom was always there for me, and for that I will always be thankful.

My dad was less than supportive. Not that he was malicious; he just didn't understand, and quite honestly I don't think he tried to. He always used to yell at me, "Why don't you just stop this habit of yours?" If it were that simple, I wouldn't be here telling my story to you. None of us would be here. I remember wearing a cloth headband to cover my bald spots as best I could. I wasn't fooling anyone, but it made me feel better. I had worn it day after day, to the point where I had to stitch it back together multiple times. One day, as I sat at the table stitching it back together for the umpteenth time, he threatened to take it and throw it in the trash. I remember sitting on my bed that night, with a lap full of hair. Thanks, Dad.

Now, I don't want you think that trich is *all* bad. Sure, there are some pretty crappy parts of it—the lack of self-esteem, the body image issues, the bouts of depression, the never feeling pretty, and always feeling like a failure because the one thing that your family wants you to stop, you cannot find a way to stop. *But*, I have learned who my true friends are. I have several friends who have been my friends since before I started pulling and are still very close to me to this day. When everyone wanted to run away from me in fear, they were usually the ones running to me to comfort me.

Having trich certainly affected my love life, but just as I learned who my true friends are, I learned which guys were superficial and not worthy of my affection. I had a few serious boyfriends growing up, and was even married for 11 years. (That's whole different conversation!) So, no, I was not prom queen. I was not Miss Popular. But I stayed true to myself, made the best of things and never let my hair define me.

I joined an online support group through Facebook a year and a half ago. At the time, there were almost 1,000 members in the group. I was shocked to see that there are so many of us out there. For so long, I felt completely alone. Now I have a worldwide family, and we truly support each other in our progresses, and we pick each other up during our failures.

August 12, 2012: I was in the middle of one of my worst pulling cycles in my adult life. My youngest daughter, Cosette, who was three years old at the time, watched me pluck a hair from my scalp as I stood in front of the computer. She asked me, "Mommy, what are you doing?" She was completely right. What WAS I doing? At that moment, I logged onto the Facebook group, and typed three simple words that would forever change my life: *I Need Help.*

That day was the first time I ever reached out for help on my own without being urged by others. Immediately I was welcomed with support and encouraging words, and the comfort of others reminding me that I am not alone in this battle. Literally, a minute after I posted that I realized I had made it a full minute pull free...then five...then ten... then an hour... I was always "checking in" to show everyone, especially myself, how well I was doing. As of today, I am 469 days pull free. I still have urges every day, but they are very fleeting, and much less intense. As time progresses, they have almost become unnoticeable.

But that is not the best part. Sure, it's wonderful that I have somehow figured out how to stop, but it also brought me a purpose in life. I have started to coach others all over the world, sharing the methods and techniques that have worked for me. I have met so many amazing people from all the corners of the earth. And I have even started a monthly support group in my area for trichsters and their support persons.

But that's still not the best part. What would you say if I told you that my trichotillomania has brought me to the love of my life? Well, it has. One day in October, 2012, Michael[4] joined the group. I remember responding to a positive post of his with an exuberant "Wooohoooooo!" We continued to "Wooohoooooo!" each other, and became close friends, supporting each other every day in our journey. Well, as luck would have it, on April Fool's Day, 2013, this man rode his Harley 400 miles to meet me. We've been in love ever since. The amazing part is that we both completely understand each other, and support each other, and together, we are helping others. We say that we are "changing the world, one head at a time" and have become the official trich couple.

I cannot predict my future. I can, however, tell you that I am hoping to somehow go back to college and become a Licensed Practicing

---

[4] Name changed to protect this person's identity.

Counselor so that I can help others professionally with their trich, as well as Dermatillomania (skin picking) Onychophagia (nail biting) and other BFRB's (Body Focused Repetitive Behaviors). As for Michael and I—well our story is nowhere near over. I am sure there is marriage in our future, one day. What can I say? I guess love can be "trichy!"

Here are the tips that I share with my fellow trichsters:

Christina's Amazing TIPS (AKA what I've learned along the way)

1. ASK for help. When you have a trigger, reach out to someone who has been there, and can help you fight it.
2. NEVER be alone, if you can help it. When you are alone and having a hard time, remember there are always people (like me) who are more than willing to be there for you, especially because we understand.
3. EDUCATE others about your trich. I know it sounds crazy, and extremely hard, but the more people you tell, the less shame you feel. At most, you may get one or two questions, (usually "doesn't it hurt?") and then it's over. And you can walk away with less weight on your shoulders.
4. FIND your "why." Why do you want to be pull/pick free? This reason will help you remain focused when you are having your urges.
5. DISCOVER what triggers you to have an urge. Boredom? Stress? Certain people? The more you know about yourself, the better you will be able to deal with the urges. I've used this analogy with others—You wouldn't go to battle without knowing the enemy. Learn your enemy.
6. CELEBRATE the small victories. Because small victories lead to huge accomplishments. I have also used this analogy—If you are running a marathon, you are not going to focus on the 26.2 miles you have to go. Instead, you learn to focus from mile marker to mile marker. That's what you need to do. Instead of focusing on being trich free forever, let's start with an hour. Then two. Then a day. You can finish that marathon, but do it little by little.
7. BREATHE. When things get really tough, it helped me to find a quiet spot (I have 3 kids so that can be tough) and close my eyes, and just breathe, slowly. Listen to your heartbeat. Listen to the air going in and out of your lungs. While you do this, imagine yourself trich free. The mind is *very* powerful.
8. DON'T strive for perfection. There may be a time when you pull a hair out here and there. But you know what? No one is perfect. Instead remember how far you've come, and realize that you have the strength to go even further.

9. MAINTAIN. Once your hair starts to grow in, cut is short and keep it short. It's much harder to hide bald spots when your hair isn't long enough to cover it.

There is a brush available at Sally Beauty supply. It costs a whopping 79 cents. It's small, and portable, and I use it to "brush" away my urges. It's called a pocket brush. I highly recommend trying it if you are a scalp puller.

Hope this helps!

*I can be contacted on Twitter: @Njtrichgirl or trichcoach@yahoo.com

14
CLAIMING YOUR HONORED SPACE
ANDY, LATE FORTIES, ILLINOIS

"If you want to keep a secret, you must also hide it from yourself." —*George Orwell*

I f you were to walk down any busy street in America and pick a person at random, you might ask them if they had any big secrets. If they were willing to talk to you, (you are a total stranger after all), they, in all likelihood, would tell you no, and believe it with every fiber of their being. And then you would both go on your merry way. We all like to believe that. But in a half an hour, or an hour, once they have gotten to where they were going, the question would likely rear up out of the subconscious and beg to be answered truthfully. Well, they would then think, there is that one.

No matter who you are, rich or poor, from a small town or a thriving metropolis, young or old, happy or cranky, we all have secrets. The things that make for a juicy novel, like stealing, cheating, lying about how many men you have dated, your real weight, how much caffeine you drink, people you have had a crush on, that you love to listen to *Air Supply*, that you would join a circus if you didn't need to pay bills at the end of the week. Mine, you ask? Well…I pull my hair.

It was 1985, I was 18, a sophomore in college at the University of Illinois. I was in my office at Carson's, a department store, as I was a poor college student, and usually held down two jobs at a time. I had been burning the candle at both ends, and a few places in the middle. I had a full, happy life, though, great friends, a full social life, great classes, a rotation of nice boys to date, a small but clean apartment, modeling gigs, intramural volleyball and basketball, and jobs that I actually loved. One of the jobs was at a movie theater, the other as a special events and fashion show coordinator at the above mentioned department store. I could have used a little more sleep, and a few more groceries, but all in all I wouldn't have asked for anything else in my life.

But on this one fall day, as I was sitting at my desk, organizing an event, I glance down at the floor, looking at something that looked a little like coiled up fishing line. What on earth? I then realized it was hair, my hair. Why was there a little pile of my hair on the floor? I did not have any memory of pulling it out, but knew that somehow I had. I was horrified. When I looked in the mirror, it wasn't noticeable, so I thought it was an aberration. I vowed to go for a run after work, to de-stress. I let it go, or so I thought. That was the first time, but certainly not the last.

In the next few months, I found other little piles of hair. And then, I created my first bald spot. It was on the back of my head, near the crown, on the right. I tried to cover it up with my shoulder length hair, and hoped that I had. But I was meeting friends for dinner, and a friend came up to me to ask if everything was all right. 'Why," I asked. "You have a bald spot on your head," he replied, with a demeanor of grave concern. I will never forget that moment for as long as I live. I completely lost my breath, and had to work to get oxygen back into my lungs. I pasted a smile on my face, and made up some ridiculous excuse, which I cannot remember anymore.

I could not figure out why a fairly bright girl would do something like this to herself, so I did what fairly bright girls do. I headed straight to the library. I pulled out books on psychology, and medicine, and before I knew it, I had a stack of about 15 large books laid out open on the gleaming wood table. I was getting close, but about to give up for the day, when I came upon three lines in a medical journal. It wasn't much, but it gave me a name, trichotillomania. Which, for the record, is a horrible, horrible, name. I had a moment's relief, and then felt nothing but horror. I had what?!?

For years after that, I could not find any more information about trich, and began to accept that this was a part of my life. I could overcome this at any time, I thought, if I just had less stress, more money, a perfect life. But life, as you know, is not perfect, and 29 years have passed since that day in my office. I have stopped pulling for short periods of time, once for almost a year, and it has grown in, and then been ravaged, repeatedly, over the years. When I was 27, I seemed to be going through a transitional phase in my life, and my hair was in fairly good shape at this point. In honor of not having much to cover it up for once, I got my regularly longish hair cut in a shoulder length bob. I was happily single, had a job I loved, traveled extensively, life was pretty good. I was flying back and forth to Houston, Texas to train a new manager, when I met a tall, brilliant, gorgeous cowboy on one of my trips. I was feeling pretty confident because I thought you couldn't really tell that I pulled my hair. I think that this was when I adopted the theory that this was something I did, a behavior, not something I was, part of my personality. It may be naive, but I think that this has helped me cope with this for all of these years.

So cowboy becomes boyfriend, and within 4 months, had moved up to Illinois, where I lived, and becomes fiancé. One year later, he becomes husband, and we have had 19 wonderful years together so far. When you keep a secret like this, you live in constant fear. Secrets have a way of being a living thing, growing in time, ready for surprising you at the worst possible moment. I told him about the trich the month that we got engaged, as I don't like those kinds of surprises. He shocked me with the information that he already knew about it, almost from the first day we met. So much for keeping my big secret. He doesn't seem to mind, although I personally hate it as much today as I did when I put a name to it that day in the library.

As I have gone along my trich journey, there have been several milestones that bear mentioning. In 1991, the Trichotillomania Learning Center, TLC, was founded. I joined the organization in 1996, when I first discovered it. They have been instrumental in "normalizing" this for me, through large quantities of literature and information. I finally had the courage to attend a TLC sponsored seminar in 2003, and although I was in a cold sweat, I girded my loins, got out of the car, and walked into the building where the mini conference was being held. There were about 100 people there, and every last one of us had this affliction. We ranged in age from 10 to 90, it seemed, and most of us had a deer in the headlights look about us, wary of raising our hands and shouting out loud that we pulled our hair out. As if that might be expected somehow. But Christina Pearson, the founder, came out, and her energy was calm and peaceful. You could almost feel the blood pressure in the room go down, collectively. It was lovely to be around all of these normal looking people, who also had trich.

Then, in 2000, I found out I was pregnant with our first child. At the first visit with my obstetrician, there was a little confusion about my due date, so they took an ultrasound. And my life changed yet again, when they discovered what they thought was a cancerous tumor on my right ovary, as big as a grapefruit. So began our journey through both oncology and obstetrics, simultaneously. We scheduled the surgery for July, when I would be about 4 and ½ months in gestation. It would give both of us the best chance at survival.

I have to say that during my pregnancy, whether it was the hormones, or the overriding fear for our unborn child, my hair pulling urge was pretty low. We made it to the surgery date, and our daughter and I both survived the surgery, which I endured without any pain medication, for the baby's sake. We then found out that the large tumor was not actually cancerous, and that the heavy suturing they used because I was pregnant caused a life threatening infection. They drilled two holes in my scar, and let me drain for the next four months, pus and suturing coming out daily. I was doubled up in pain on the floor every night, trying to keep our baby in there, and alive. I haven't had a pain free day since, 13 years of them in total.

On December 1, 2000, I went into labor, and 29 hours later, after she got stuck in the birth canal, and her heart rate plummeted, our daughter was brought into this world. It was December 3. Another post-surgical infection ensued, and I was so sick that I thought I was going to die. I was so happy that she had 10 fingers, and 10 toes, and that she was a normal weight and beautiful, that I didn't even notice the crushing pain even lower in my abdomen. Eventually we found out that she had been left too long in the canal, crushing nerves in the right iliosacral joint. According to multiple doctors, I am lucky to have avoided paralysis and a wheelchair. Well, luck is in the eye of the beholder, and I can say that I am grateful for many things in my life.

Our daughter is a healthy, brilliant, and beautiful 13 year old, seventh grader. My husband has supported me in so many ways, large and small, through 10 surgeries, tears and keening at 3:00 a.m., depression, feelings of inadequacy, and the ever increasing desire to pull my hair. He and our daughter were at the finish line a couple of months ago, when I finished my first marathon. I heard repeatedly from doctors that I should give up on running, or the gym, or being an athlete in general, that I would be lucky not to end up bedridden.

I have learned how strong I am. They cannot tell me what I am or am not capable of, who I am at my core. I have learned what the mind and body can do in the darkest, most naked moments, when it is you and life and death, at its' most elemental and primitive. But, the price for that survival has been often times at the cost of my stamina, my fearlessness, my sense of humor, my patience, my weight, and my hair follicle count.

Doesn't It Hurt?

I have learned that there are lessons in tragedy. Regardless of the scars that criss- cross my body, and my sometimes balding scalp, my spine is more than strong enough to withstand anything life can throw at me. In the last month, I had to have my face cut in half, to remove a cancerous basal cell carcinoma by the left side of my nose. Just when I thought that I could not take one more cancer scare, or one more hit to my vanity, I found out that apparently, I could. After the swelling went down, and the black and blue marks faded, I was left with a three-inch scar down my face. But when I looked in the mirror this week, the line is fading to white, and the cancer is gone. The plastic surgeon did a good job. My skin is still beautiful and almost completely unlined for 47, my freckles are the same as when I was a girl, and my smile is almost back to normal. My husband says he digs scars, and I choose to believe him. Beauty can be largely mental, and if I own the entrance to a room just as I did when I was younger, then the outcome is the same.

I have learned that the people I have trusted with my dual secrets of trich and chronic pain were more than worthy of the honor, and that I am blessed to have them for friends and family. I was wise or lucky or both when I chose my lifelong friends along the way. It is very comforting to know that we have each other's back.

I have learned that progress can very often times look like a bunch of failures, because it can take failure after failure before we learn enough to overcome our demons, whatever they may be. You can't let it break you, because the reward for persistence is too great.

I have learned that after hearing repeatedly that the payoff, if there is one, for pulling sessions, is that when we go into a pulling trance, it is soothing. But I had a pretty bad pulling session recently, and while it was going on, I had checked out of my head. At the end of the day, I checked back in, I mean really checked back in, not a slow gradual check in. I asked myself for the first time ever, was I soothed? And the answer, in all honestly, and surprisingly, was no, it did not soothe me at all. And to add insult to injury, I looked in the mirror, and felt immense sadness. If there is absolutely no payoff, then maybe I can identify more easily when I am in a zone for starting, and find something that would give me the payoff I am actually seeking. Because isn't that what we all want at the end of the day, to find peace and acceptance?

I have learned some coping techniques that have helped me survive the years with trich as a companion. First, that buying a wig should be one of those rare times when money is no object. A great wig can be the difference between fretting about your head constantly, and occasionally forgetting you even deal with this on a daily basis.

Second, don't be mean to yourself. There should be no name calling. It's just hair. It grows back. It doesn't keep you from seeing the beautiful sunsets, or your child's first smile, or the miracles of everyday life.

Third, when you have a pulling episode, it can be over when it's over. It is not permission to string episode after episode together in a row.

Fourth, learn to pay attention to your body's voice. When it tells you that it needs something to calm it down, tune in. Meditation, running, music. Whatever brings you peace. Find the key to the lock of what brings you joy, and do more of it. For me, those include basketball, baking cookies and pies, running races, reading, lunch and old movies with friends. More of it, more of it, more of it.

Fifth, find the things that make you feel anxious and stressed, and do what you can to lessen their importance. Not do away with them, that is simply not realistic, but lessen their importance, as they set the platform for most pulling episodes.

And finally, this world is beautiful and tragic. Loved ones are born and loved ones die. Awards are won, keys are lost. We hurt each other, love each other, sit with our precious grandmothers as they lay dying, buy Prom dresses, climb the mountain, fall to our knees in failure. We take chances, buy gifts, smell the spring air, watch the harvest, wreck our cars. We see shooting stars, lose the game for our team, smell our babies' hair, watch towers fall. We smell buttered popcorn, get trapped in a snowstorm, take photographs, survive rape, go on trips with our best friends. Pay attention. There is magic in the small spaces of life. Find your honored space, and claim it. Don't take no for an answer.

*I can be contacted here: APL32@aol.com

15
WHAT THE PLUCK
SANDY, LATE THIRTIES, MARYLAND

All of us have secrets.

We learn to live with them. We usually keep them close. And of all of them, there's usually one biggie. One we hope and pray will never be discovered.

But if others did discover our secret, what are we so afraid would happen? Why do we hold the secret so tightly against our chests?

Every day I go to great lengths to hide what I really look like. I've lived in extreme shame because I have a disorder that an estimated 2-4 percent of the nation has. Few know about it, and even fewer are willing to talk about it.

I've been living with **trichotillomania (trich for short) for 32 years.** Trich is a disorder that causes people to **pull hair from the face,** underarms, beard, chest, legs, pubic area, or other parts of the body. Hair pulling varies greatly in severity and location, but many times it results in noticeable bald patches. Many who suffer from it go through phases in which it presents as very severe, while in others it is barely noticeable at all.

I pull out my upper eyelashes.

I used to believe that if people noticed or if I shared this fact, they would stop liking or loving me. I was sure they would judge me and tell others what a freak I was. I did everything in my power to make sure no one would ever notice. My worst phase was between the ages of 7-11.

When I was seven, my parents got a divorce. My father moved out of the house and my concept of family was shattered. I began to pull. I had no idea what I was doing or why; I just knew it felt good.

The first time I pulled I was looking into my playroom mirror, studying my face. As a seven year old I was fascinated by all parts of my body, especially my face. I'm not sure what compelled me to reach towards my eyes, but I did. I began to feel my eyelashes between my fingers. I felt the texture, the softness, the vulnerability of a single strand of hair, and then ... PLUCK. I pulled one out of my eyelids. There was something satisfying about the feeling. There was something in the power and pain of it, the simultaneous act of creation and destruction. It was a moment that changed me, defined me, and shaped me into the person I am today. It was that day that began my downward spiral.

At first no one noticed. My secret was still safe. Then, little by little, tiny bald patches appeared on my head. Little by little, I had fewer eyelashes and eyebrows.

At some point my parents began to notice. This is how my father describes the first moment he saw that I'd been pulling:

> I very clearly remember coming to visit my children one evening when Sandy was about 7 or 8 and my ex-wife pulling me aside when I first arrived. She asked me if I knew Sandy was mutilating herself. I was stunned. This couldn't be. I loved my children more than anything in the world. They were beautiful. (They still are.) Self-mutilation—my daughter—it just didn't register. And then I went to see Sandy in her room and my wife showed me a bald spot on her head, partially hidden by long straight hair but about the circumference of a baseball. And her eyelashes and eyebrows were mostly gone. I felt like I was punched in the stomach.

My parents asked me why I was pulling. I was seven, for God's sake—how was this once bubbly, energetic, and innocent little girl supposed to explain the sudden self-destruction, the sudden desecration of her own body?

I had no answer for them. They took me to doctors and psychiatrists, only to find that there was no explanation for why the disorder starts and that for most people, there is no cure. (There are treatment options, but as of 2014, most with the disorder will not be cured.

Many of us living with it know we will always have to battle this.)

Then, just as my parents began to have me see a doctor regularly in hopes of ending what many see as self-mutilation, the kids at my school began to notice. They stopped playing with me and began calling me a freak. I started to dread taking the school bus, as I never knew when the older kids would bully me, calling me ugly or chanting, "What's wrong with you, freak?"

Sometimes they pushed me down the aisle or onto the floor, and sometimes they kicked me while I was down there. At one point these same kids came to my house and asked me to come out and play. I was thrilled; I thought maybe they'd changed their minds and I was actually being accepted (oh, the innocent mind of a second grader). Instead, they took me around the corner to beat me up.

I longed to have someone like me to talk to, cry with, to share the hurt and shame. Someone who would understand what I was going through. I wanted someone who would get it, get me, see me—the real me.

Instead, I was alone.

As a child, I used to love being in photographs. But around this time, I began to want fewer and fewer of them taken of me. I couldn't even look at the photos my parents hung on the walls. I also stopped looking in mirrors. I knew who would be there staring back at me—that person everyone called freak. The girl that had something wrong with her. Why would I want to look at her? No one else did.

When I was old enough, I took those photos down and hid them. I asked my family to never take them out. I never wanted to see them again. Why would I want to be reminded of a time in my life with such painful memories attached? My family obliged. My plan was to never in my lifetime ever see those photos again.

As I got older, a few people began to notice my lack of eyelashes. If they didn't ask, I knew they'd seen it by the look they gave me. When they did ask, I took a deep breath and wished the conversation away. When that failed and questions still hung, unanswered, I told the truth. More times than not, I received positive responses. Many people shared something they too had held close to them, which they now felt safe to share with me. We connected over our deeply held, often shameful secrets. Twice, people shared that they also had trich.

If you know someone with **trich** or you're reading this and finding yourself wanting to ask me, *why don't you just stop?* – please don't. It's a question many of us who have the disorder ask ourselves on a daily basis. When asked by someone else, we usually just wait uncomfortably for the subject to change. Here is the answer: *We don't know.* Most of us will never be able to stop. If we could, we would.

As I reluctantly told others about my own battle with trich, despite getting positive responses that were the complete opposite of what I had anticipated (including discovering that others in my own life walked around with the same shame as me), I still didn't feel safe sharing my secret. In serious relationships with men in particular, I hid it for as long as possible. When they did find out, I prayed they wouldn't leave me. They never did. But even knowing that people were accepting, I still wasn't ready to really share. I was holding onto those few negative responses from when I was a girl. I couldn't let go of them, and they were running my show.

At 38, I have no eyelashes on my upper eyelids. I pull them out whenever I'm anxious, sad or stressed. Each morning I spend at least ten minutes meticulously applying heavy black eyeliner before I face the world, so that no one will notice that I don't have real eyelashes. Applying it has become an art form. As a young woman, when I slept over at someone's house, I washed my face but never removed my eyeliner. In fact, I woke up in the middle of the night just to reapply it so that in the morning it would be just as perfect as when I fell asleep. That habit carried over into adulthood, and when I'm in a relationship, I find myself sneaking out of bed in the middle of the night to reapply it, so he won't see me without it.

I'm not exactly sure what changed or why, but one day I decided I was going to test the waters. I started by telling just a few friends that I had trich. Trusted friends. Every single one was one hundred percent accepting, and yet again I found that my sharing gave others the opportunity to share. They told me secrets they had always feared revealing. They shared of themselves.

This got me thinking. Whenever I shared my secret, I created an opportunity for those closest to me to share theirs. Simply by being honest, I created a space for them to get something off of their chests they'd been holding for years. I never saw it coming, but it was beautiful when it did.

I began to get a little bolder. I stood up in a two hundred-person seminar in which the topic was self-development and brain patterns and shared my secret yet again. The instructor actually thanked me and went on to explain to everyone that at some point during my childhood when my brain patterns formed, probably after a traumatic event, I began to pull my hair, and it became a more ingrained pattern. He was grateful I'd spoken up, since it was an excellent example of the lesson he was teaching. And significantly, on the next break, quite a few people hugged me, thanked me, and again shared something.

There it was again: an opportunity to connect with others.

I still wasn't ready to share with everyone, but I found myself telling more and more people. Finally, something came over me. I decided to go for it. I wrote an article and submitted it to *The Huffington Post*—the most public of forums I could think of (after all, once something is on the *Internet*, it's out forever).

I'm still not really sure what prompted me to make that decision. Maybe I was guided by something greater than myself. Maybe I was just ready. At any rate, once I submitted it, my nerves got the best of me. The same negative chatter spun in my head: What if people didn't like or love me? What if they judged me or, even worse, told others what a freak I was? If published, it would be irreversible. When people Googled me, it would be one of the first things they'd find. My secret would become public knowledge.

As I peeled back the negative layers, I noticed I was still nervous. Why? If it wasn't that I was scared of being judged, what was it?

That's when I realized: I was even more nervous that my article *wouldn't* be published. I was afraid no one would ever read my words, that others living with trich would still feel utterly alone. *I realized that I wanted to share because it was an opportunity.*

A few days later I got the news. My story was going to be published! Not only that—it was going to be featured on the homepage of AOL! I cried. I was elated and proud. And what followed next I could have never predicted.

As soon as the article came out, friends who'd never known my secret called, texted and emailed. They said I was beautiful, even brave. At least five said they'd been living with the same disorder, also in fear and shame. Three had never told anyone before me. Again, my sharing had opened up a space. They knew I would love, accept, and understand them, and never judge them.

I had no idea the larger impact that would come of my piece. People from all over the United States read it, as did those from the UK, Sweden, Canada, Australia and Ireland. The comments under the article

121

itself were beautiful. Many resonated with what I'd written, and shared this could have been their own story. I was thanked for being the voice people couldn't utter themselves.

But perhaps the most meaningful connections came from mothers who found me on Facebook, asking me to speak with their teenage daughters. Their girls with trich were shutting them out because they felt their mothers would "never understand," and the mothers were desperate for someone to get through to them. I now speak to quite a few of these girls. Really, all I provide them is the chance to feel they're not alone, the opportunity to feel understood.

That's what I realized what I was also providing to a wider audience: a tribe. I was the start of a community for those who had felt lonely, misunderstood, disliked, and worst of all, unloved from the shame they were carrying. Speaking my own truth had given others the opportunity to speak theirs, to feel loved and share themselves with people from all over the world. I was stunned. *I* had done that.

For most of my life, I lived in fear of others discovering my secret. I, like many others, carried a lot of shame. I was ashamed of the hairlessness and ashamed I couldn't stop. I was ashamed I wanted to hide it.

And I made the whole thing mean something about myself. I made it mean that I'm ugly, unworthy, unlikeable, and unlovable. This is a story I began telling myself when I was seven years old, before things began to change.

My path was not always smooth. I went through my 20s and most of my 30s consciously, deliberately, determinedly not facing my past, not even wanting to look there. It wasn't so much that I was afraid as that I simply wasn't willing to do it. Quite frankly, I didn't want to. I wanted to just move on and pretend it wasn't a part of me. I just wanted it to be over.

But little by little, perhaps without me even realizing it, I grew up. I grew into myself. Maybe I grew beyond who I was before. I don't know. I do know that as I have grown into a woman I love, I decided to do what I promised myself I would never do: face my past. Sure, I had talked about it, told the same stories ad nauseum, complained about it, but I hadn't really *identified* with it. Intuitively I knew this was related to actually looking at pictures from my youth, pictures I'd made my parents take down, take away.

Recently, I chose to no longer avoid what I had kept hidden away for so long.

It was a decision born of the intuitive sense that maybe (OK, likely) there was something there for me. I didn't know exactly what. A connection to the past, perhaps? An admission that I had really lived through that, that now I was different—or that in reality I was still the same? Whatever it was, even after I decided to do it, it took me weeks to muster up the courage to actually look at the photographs.

Finally, one night, I sat with them.

I studied them for hours.

And one question kept echoing in my mind:

Who was this little girl I was looking at?

I was looking at a little girl who loved to roller-skate with her dad. I was looking at a little girl who loved riding her bike. I was looking at a little girl who used to jump rope with her sister, with two ponytails in her hair that her mother tied with ribbons. I was looking at a little girl who was told she was ugly, that she was a freak, that there was something wrong with her. I was looking at a little girl who at some point decided that what everyone else said (aside from her parents and grandmother) was true.

In other words, I was looking at me, and the time in my life when I made a choice. I chose my story: I am ugly. I am unworthy. I am unlikeable. Worst of all, I am unlovable. I chose to live that story for a portion of my life while doing everything I could to prove otherwise. I worked hard to distract people, to make them like me even though I knew I was unlikeable, to make them love me even though I knew I was unlovable.

I believed my story. And I lived it out, every day.

But what I realized, looking at those photos again, reliving those memories, was that it was always just a story. It wasn't "true;" it was something I made up. Not only that, but I made it up when I was *seven*.

That story I wrote as a young girl who didn't really know any better but was doing the best she could, was fiction. As an adult, strong and conscious, I found that the story I'd gone around telling myself and others for years … simply wasn't true.

I believe the stories we tell ourselves create our lives. They don't necessarily create the circumstances (although they do affect them in deep and profound ways), but they create our experience of our lives. So even if I'd been loved, *I hadn't felt loved*, because I had the story that I was unlovable. And even if I'd been told I was beautiful, *I didn't believe I was beautiful*, because in my story I was ugly.

So here's a different story: I am a beautiful, passionate, loving woman who will do anything for the people she loves. I am authentic with myself and with others, even when it's uncomfortable or nerve-wracking. I am a person open to learning and growing.

I am a human being, alive and vulnerable and true.

*I can be contacted on Twitter: @sandybeach28 or www.myopportunityis.com/trichotillomania-hair-pulling

EPILOGUE

Is Trich An Opportunity?

Those of us who live with trich know how difficult it is to not pull. To go one day pull-free—even just one day—is amazing. It's a *success*. It's also a feat that should be applauded.

We all know how hard it is. Maybe it's the beginning of never pulling again. However, it may not be. And rather than taking the time to "pick/pull apart" the drama of what happened, what went wrong, what you did wrong, or what is wrong with you, what if we all just took that moment to celebrate?

Yes, I said CELEBRATE.

For every day you live pull-free, I want you to celebrate. And if you pull again, whether it's two days, two weeks, or two years later, the next pull-free day that comes around, I want you to celebrate that, too! Any day we can say, "Hey! I did it. I really did it," is a day that calls for celebration.

I don't mean a brief pat on the back. Actually take a moment, sit down, and compliment yourself. Show yourself some love. Acknowledge yourself for every hard moment and every day that went by that you struggled and yet *you did not pull.*

Celebrate the fact that there is something really fabulous about you, and that you accomplished what many have not been able to and some may never do. Perhaps this is just the beginning. Maybe just maybe the next time you go pull-free, you'll go even longer.

No matter who we are or what we do in life, there will be moments when we will fall off the horse. It doesn't matter how many lessons we took, or how good we are at riding. We *will* fall off. So rather than beating ourselves for falling off, why don't we pick ourselves up off of the ground, dust ourselves off, and hop back on?

It's not about the falling. It's about the getting back up.

Always has been.

***

While there are days when I struggle with the same negative voices I used to hear so often, now there is another voice. It is the voice that tells me that who I am is a gift. It says that sharing my story is a gift. It reminds me that I am not only a gift to my loved ones, but to the larger community of people who need someone like me to speak up and show the world that we are a group of amazing individuals.

We happen to have a disorder in which we pull out our hair. So what? Underneath that, we're human beings: flawed, blundering, ashamed, hopeful, sensitive, often misunderstood, sometimes deeply understood, and beautiful. And without that same disorder, I might not have had the chance to remind both others and myself that this is who I am. Who we are.

So I am here to let you know that you are perfect exactly like you are AND exactly like you are not.

I am here to listen and share my story.

I am here to be the person I always wished I had had in my life.

I am here to eradicate shame around Trichotillomania.

I am here to step into the shoes I was always meant to wear.

I am here to love myself and all of you.

I was meant to be a voice. Today, I am that voice. *We* are that voice. The Voice of Trichotillomania.

That is our real story.

So: is trichotillomania an opportunity?

Yes. It is.

Take advantage of it!

Sandy Rosenblatt

A portion of the proceeds for this book will be donated to:

The Trichotillomania Learning Center. Founded in 1991, the Trichotillomania Learning Center (TLC) is a nonprofit organization devoted to ending the suffering caused by hair pulling disorder, skin picking disorder, and related body-focused repetitive behaviors. TLC provides education, outreach, and support of research into the cause and treatment of BFRB disorders. TLC assists thousands of people each month with treatment referrals, support communities, educational events, and much more. Working with a Scientific Advisory Board of the world's leading researchers & clinicians, TLC provides best-practice training programs for therapeutic professionals, and funds research to find a cure for BFRBs.

TLC envisions a world where:

- Body-focused Repetitive Behaviors (BFRBs) are diagnosed quickly.
- BFRBs are not a source of shame.
- Knowledgeable treatment is available to all people with these disorders.
- Treatments are more effective and eventually cures are found.
- Information and emotional support are available to people of all ages and their families.

Compulsive hair pulling and skin picking are disorders that cause millions of people to live in shame and isolation. TLC transforms the lives of sufferers and their families by providing hope, support, and recovery.

For more information, or to get involved, please visit www.trich.org. Or contact TLC at Twitter: @tlcBFRB.

Canadian BFRB Support Network (CBSN). CBSN is Canada's leading educational resource for hair pullers, skin pickers, and professionals alike. CBSN or Canadian Body Focused Repetitive Behaviour Support Network is Canada's leading support network and educational resource for hair pullers, skin pickers, loved ones, and professionals alike.

Headquartered in Toronto, Ontario the Canadian BFRB Support Network (CBSN) is a federally registered non-profit organization and upcoming charitable Canadian organization. It aims to provide support and educational resources for those with Body-Focused Repetitive Behaviours

(BFRBs) as well as **reduce the stigma, shame, and isolation** associated with BFRBs and related mental health conditions. BFRB is an umbrella term for conditions such as Trichotillomania aka Hair Pulling Disorder, and Dermatillomania aka Skin Picking (Excoriation) Disorder.

They are the second organization of its kind in the world, and Canada's leading support and educational resource for Canadian pullers, pickers and professionals alike.

Learn more at www.canadianbfrb.org.
Or contact CBSN at Twitter: @CanadianBFRB.

ACKNOWLEDGEMENTS

Special thanks to cover artist, Viviana Rouco, as well as Mike and Jasmin Morrell

ABOUT THE EDITOR

Sandy has been living with trichotillomania since the age of 7.

She is a writer, blogger and speaker who is passionate about eradicating shame around trich as well as other body focused repetitive behaviors (BFRBs). Sandy has been featured in *Huffington Post, Huffington Post Live, AOL News, US World News and Report, The Sydney Morning Herald, YourTango, New York Daily News,* and *Inforum.* She has also had the honor of speaking on The Success Panel at the Trichotillomania Learning Center's 2013 Annual Conference.

Sandy is a voice for those living with trich, supporting them to lead the extraordinary lives that they desire to lead, as well as educating those that are unfamiliar with the disorder.

Sandy sees her life as a journey. She enjoys her family, friends, nature, exercise, living life authentically and is a lover of animals. She cannot resist a good pun. Sandy loves spending time with her niece & nephew as well as her cats. She believes that everyone has a gift and loves that she can make a difference in people's lives.

Find out more at www.myopportunityis.com/trichotillomania-hair-pulling and tweet her @sandybeach28.

Made in the USA
Middletown, DE
05 May 2017